THEY KEPT ME LOYAL
TO THE YANKEES

THEY KEPT ME LOYAL TO THE YANKEES

Vic Debs

RUTLEDGE HILL PRESS
Nashville, Tennessee

Published in Nashville, Tennessee, by Rutledge Hill Press, 211 Seventh Avenue North, Nashville, Tennessee 37219

Typography by D&T/Bailey, Nashville, Tennessee

Library of Congress Cataloging-in-Publication Data

Debs, Victor, 1949–
    They kept me loyal to the Yankees / Victor Debs.
      p.   cm.
    Includes index.
    ISBN 1-55853-225-0
    1. New York Yankees (Baseball team)—History. 2. Baseball players—United States—Biography. I. Title.
    GV875.N4D43   1993
    792.357'64'097471—dc20   93-14774
                                          CIP

Printed in the United States of America
1 2 3 4 5 6 7 8—99 98 97 96 95 94 93

To Lola and Jackie
My best friends

CONTENTS

ACKNOWLEDGEMENTS

A PUBLISHED WORK IS RARELY THE result of a solo effort, and this one is far from being an exception. I'd like to thank the following organizations and people for helping make this book possible:

To the patient staff at the research department of the St. George Library, Staten Island, for their help in locating microfilm; to Milo Stewart of the National Baseball Library, Fred Cantey of the Associated Press, and Barbara Mancuso of the *New York Times*, for locating the photos; and to all at Rutledge Hill Press for their diligence and dedication.

Special thanks go to the following individuals: Gary Muschla for his superb job of editing the original manuscript; Larry Stone and Ron Pitkin of Rutledge Hill Press who took a chance on a first-time author; Lou Bergonzi, sports editor of the *Staten Island Advance*; and John Holway, noted author and former publications director at the Society for American Baseball Research, for giving me my first breaks in print.

Finally, I want to thank my parents, Victor and

Sonja; my brothers Gene and Ray; and my sister, Monique, for the love, friendship, and support they've always given. And I want to thank God for sending me the two most precious people in my life: my wonderful wife, Lola, and darling daughter, Jackie. Their love and support inspire all that I do.

INTRODUCTION

THE MID-SIXTIES TO EARLY SEVENTIES was a difficult period for Americans. The civil rights movement. The King and Kennedy assassinations. Our involvement in Vietnam. Kent State. Watergate. Adults had a hard time accepting the changes that young people were demanding. Our presidents were making mistakes and shattering our faith in government. Values were becoming liberalized, leading to the sexual revolution, women's and gay rights, and legalized abortion.

In keeping with the turbulent spirit of the times, the New York Yankees began losing. Previously, one would have thought that regardless of whatever changes took place in the United States, the one unshakable, everlasting truth was that the Yankees would win the pennant annually.

Oh, there would be an occasional lapse every four or five years, but that would only be to prove to the skeptics that the pennant race wasn't rigged. The Yankees could play in the World Series whenever they had a mind to. That axiom was proved as untrue as the one that assumed that Americans would always support their government in any war without question.

The Yankees won the pennant in 1964 and would not win another one for the next eleven seasons. What made it difficult for players and fans alike was that throughout most of those years, the Bombers were not even contenders. Except for a couple of seasons, the Yankees were consistently out of the pennant race by the All-Star break. The Twins, Orioles, Red Sox, Tigers, and A's were taking turns playing in the Fall Classic against the National League challengers. New York, to the delight of rival American Leaguers, had gone into hibernation and would not come out of it until the dawn of the Billy Martin era in the mid-seventies.

A look at the Yankee record and place in the standings after each season from 1965 to 1975 points out their turnabout from the glory days of Yankee dynasties.

Year	Place in Standings	Won–Lost Record
1965	sixth*	77–85
1966	tenth*	70–89
1967	ninth*	72–90
1968	fifth*	83–79
1969	fifth*	80–81
1970	second**	93–69
1971	fourth**	82–80
1972	fourth**	79–76
1973	fourth**	80–82
1974	second**	89–73
1975	third**	83–77

*Denotes no divisional play
**Denotes divisional play

The losses must have been especially hard on Yankee heroes of the mid-sixties. Stars like Roger Maris, Elston Howard, Joe Pepitone, and Tom Tresh, all of whom had had a taste of the World Series, found themselves on a team that could no longer challenge. Mickey Mantle was even more familiar with post-season play, and the only thing that kept him going through all the losses and injuries he sustained was his immense pride in his performance and the overwhelming admiration of the fans. The veterans couldn't stand or understand losing. Clete Boyer, commenting on the Yankees' last place finish of 1966, said, "It was frustrating as hell. It was almost unbelievable when we realized we were going to lose."

Passengers on the "unsinkable" *Titanic* must have experienced the same feelings. Sailing along with confidence on a ship believed to be invulnerable, they discovered that they were on a loser, sinking fast and unable to save the ship or themselves. But just as some fortunate passengers were rescued, some of the Yankees were lucky. They were traded to other teams, and some even went to pennant winners. Elston Howard was traded to the Red Sox in 1967, the year they won the pennant. Roger Maris was dealt to the Cardinals that same year and wound up getting another World Series ring with his new ball club. But the Yanks who remained must have wished at times that they had been on the *Titanic*.

It couldn't have been much easier for young Yanks who had been waiting for their chance at putting on the pinstripes. When newcomers Bobby Murcer, Roy White, and Horace Clarke took over, they found themselves in one losing season after another. There were some sparks now and then, like the 1970 season when the Yankees finished in second place with a 93–69 record; but that record is deceptive, for the Yankees still finished far behind the invincible Oriole team that year and were out of the pennant picture rather early. The new generation Yankees probably wondered why, in all the decades of the twentieth century, they should be destined to play for the Yanks during those years.

As hard as it must have been for the players, it couldn't have been as hard as it was for the fans. Yankee-haters didn't make it easier, either. It had always been difficult to be a Yankee fan. They were traditionally the team everyone loved to hate. (Didn't they even make a movie and Broadway play depicting just that?) Those damn Yankees! How everyone despised them when they were winning! Even in their hometown, the Yanks were the bridesmaid team in terms of popularity. The Brooklyn Dodgers (Dem Bums) and the Giants owned the hearts of most baseball fans in New York; and when those franchises deserted the Big Apple, it wasn't the Yankees that New Yorkers directed their affection toward, but the newly formed Mets. It wasn't so much that the Mets were so lovably hapless and inept on the field that made them so popular. The truth is the Mets offered New Yorkers an alternative to rooting for the Yanks.

Now that the Yankees were losing, however, Yankee critics became downright obnoxious. Fans poked affable fun at the Mets during the sixties. It was as if the more mistakes they made, the more popular they became. When the Yanks began their losing ways, the players and fans alike were subjected to sarcastic remarks by gleeful Yankee-haters. One friend who took particular delight in teasing me had derisive nicknames for some of the Yankee players. He referred to Jim Bouton as Jim "B-out-less," and Tommy Tresh as Tommy "Trash." He used to refer to Mantle as "Granpappy Amos" in reference to the way he limped around the bases the same way Walter Brennan hobbled around in the television series "The Real McCoys."

If the Bombers weren't successful as a team in that period, they still had some outstanding ball players. Starting with Mickey Mantle, the greatest player of all time, I began to follow closely the statistics of Yankee players who attracted me the most with their agility on the field, speed on the base paths, pitching prowess, or skill with the bat. None of them received the Cy Young award or Most Valuable Player award, or won a home run or batting title during those trying years; but they had outstanding ability and some pretty good seasons, good enough to make me want to follow their careers and continue following the Yankees. This book is a salute to those players who kept me loyal to the Yankees. Thanks for the memories, gentlemen!

THEY KEPT ME LOYAL
TO THE YANKEES

Mickey Mantle
[National Baseball Library, Cooperstown, New York]

CHAPTER ONE

MICKEY MANTLE

The Star Shines Brightest at Twilight

IN 1968 I SAW MICKEY MANTLE HIT ONE of his last home runs into the right-center-field bleachers in Yankee Stadium, a true Mantle shot. In his next time at bat, Mickey hit a line drive to right, which he hustled into a double, bad legs and all. (Mickey's chronic leg problems were worst during his final four seasons.) As he limped off the field for a pinch runner, the crowd gave him a thunderous standing ovation, the kind reserved for Mantle. They cheered not for the fact that an aging, almost crippled superstar would turn a single into a double, but because he was Mickey Mantle, whom they would soon see no more.

Between the years 1965 and 1968, most Yankee fans like myself didn't follow the Yankees. They followed Mickey Mantle. Whether the Yankees won or lost a particular game was insignificant. What mattered was whether Mantle hit a home run, got two or more hits, or drove in any runs. Other ball players were important only as a basis of comparison to

Mantle. During each season, we'd root for the Mick to hit for a higher average than Tony Oliva or Carl Yastrzemski, to drive in more runs than Brooks Robinson or Willie Mays, or to hit more homers than Harmon Killebrew or Frank Howard.

Mickey had everything baseball could offer a kid growing up some thirty-five years ago. He had All-American looks, was a switch-hitter, and could hit a ball farther than anyone else. Even his name is euphonious. How could a young boy hear the name Mickey Mantle and not become mesmerized by it? Like many, I grew up idolizing the Mick.

Mickey's last outstanding season was in 1964. He batted .303 with 35 home runs and 108 RBI's. The Yankees won the pennant, barely, and went on to lose the World Series in seven games to the Cardinals. Mantle finished his last World Series in typical fashion, hitting three homers, one in the ninth inning to win game three and his last off Bob Gibson. He should have won the Most Valuable Player award that year, but they gave it to Brooks Robinson. Mickey had won the award in 1956, 1957, and 1962, but no one had ever won it four times. Perhaps that's why they gave it to Brooks.

The years I remember best were Mickey's most unproductive seasons, from 1965 to 1968. It's not a coincidence that during Mantle's declining years the Yankees were sinking to a level of mediocrity. Former Yankee stalwarts such as Yogi Berra, Tony Kubek, Johnny Blanchard, and Moose Skowron were gone, and Bobby Richardson, Roger Maris, and Frank Howard were soon to follow. Pitchers weren't throwing many strikes to Mickey, and, with his leg problems, it's a miracle he performed as well as he did during his final four seasons.

Mantle started the 1965 season quite normally,

hitting four homers in April. One shot, off Camilio Pascual, came on opening day at Yankee Stadium against the Minnesota Twins, the team that won the pennant that year. With guys like Tony Oliva, Harmon Killebrew, and Bobby Allison, they bullied the Yankee pitchers that day, but it was Mickey who started the fireworks in the very first inning, parking a Pascual curve into the upper deck in right. Pascual was no match for the Mick, but he sure was for the rest of the Yankees, who were shut out for the remainder of the game.

I also remember the last homer he hit that month. In his second at bat Mickey, batting right-handed, pulled a ball into the left-field seats. The Yanks won the game 1–0 behind the superb pitching of Mel Stottlemyre, who went on to win twenty that year.

It wasn't until about two weeks later that Mickey hit his next one. The Yankees were behind by a run when Mantle came up in the third or fourth inning and singled to tie the score. His next time up, he hit a home run, again tying the score. With the Yanks trailing 3–2 in his last at bat, the Mick hit a ball to left. I'll never forget sports announcer Phil Rizzuto's excitement in anticipation of another home run as he called the shot:

"There's a drive to deep left and that ball is . . . off the top of the wall!" he said, his voice dropping in disappointment as he realized that Mickey had to settle for a double. Naturally, Mantle was stranded there, or rather, the pinch runner who replaced him was stranded, and the Yankees lost 3–2. Carl Yastrzemski drove in all the runs for the Red Sox with a pair of homers. The sports page headline in a New York paper the next day read: "Yastrzemski out-homers Mantle 2–1."

The brushback pitch is rarely used by major-league hurlers these days, but Mantle and players of his time saw it often. Here Mick goes down from a delivery by Hank Aguirre in 1966. [Photo by Ernie Sisto/New York Times]

Mantle hit another memorable home run later that year. Listening on a transistor radio as my family was driving home from Poughkeepsie, I could barely hear the call when Mickey hit a 400-foot shot off Yankee nemesis Dean Chance that went way out into the right-center-field seats.

Mantle finished the 1965 season with the worst statistics of his career to that point. Playing in 122 games, he batted .255, driving in only 46 runs and hitting a mere 19 homers. With the exception of 1963, when he played only a third of the season, it was the first time that the Mick had hit fewer than 20 four-baggers since his rookie year when he belted thirteen. The 1966 season would prove whether Mantle would rebound and once again challenge the other sluggers for the home run title. Harmon Killebrew,

Frank Robinson, Boog Powell, and Carl Yastrzemski were his greatest rivals at that time.

Mantle started the season with the same kind of frustration at the plate he had experienced the previous year. He didn't hit his first homer for nearly a month, and Mark Gallagher points out in his book, *Explosion*, that "It was the latest date of his career for his first homer—coming in his twenty-third game." Almost two months later, Mick had connected only six more times, giving him a mere seven round-trippers with the All-Star break only a few weeks away. This was the year that Frank Robinson had gotten off to a great start on his way to that fabulous triple crown year, the first player to accomplish the feat since Mantle did it in 1956.

To make matters worse, the Yankees were off to just as miserable a start, and any hopes of winning the pennant were dashed early. Yankee fans panicked. I even started turning my attention toward other stars such as Tom Tresh and Joe Pepitone, in hopes that they would be able to challenge the league leaders and keep my interest in baseball alive for the year. But it wasn't the same as rooting for the Mick.

When he exploded in early May with one of the hottest streaks of his career, it was truly satisfying. It began in late June at Fenway Park when Mantle hit two homers in each of the first two games of a three-game series. The revitalized Mick reawakened my interest in him. Could he keep it up? The third game, untelevised, would be the test.

Mickey made out a couple of times sandwiched in between three walks. I was furious. The Red Sox pitchers were not challenging the Mick very often that day. Even now, I don't agree with what they did. The Red Sox weren't doing much better than the Yanks that year, and here was a legend of the game having an infrequent batting spree during the twilight of his career. At that time, which would have been more significant to baseball and its posterity— giving Mantle a fair chance at continuing that streak or having the then-lowly Red Sox win one additional game?

Most baseball enthusiasts probably would argue that I'm seeing the game through hindsight. They might add that winning is the only thing that should matter to a team; but if that's true, then why do we keep statistics on baseball players? When Maris had a chance to break Ruth's homer record on the last day of the season, why didn't Tracy Stallard walk him in every at bat? His team's chances of winning the game probably would have been better if he had. Maybe it had something to do with class. Those who remember Roger's great achievement should also remember that Stallard had class.

Anyway, it was over as far as I was concerned. Mantle had had a brief resurgence, but his skills were too far gone to allow the streak to continue. That's what I thought after the game, but Mickey proved me wrong. The streak began all over again the next day in Washington at the start of a three-game weekend series against the Senators. He connected once on Friday and twice on Saturday, then socked another one on Sunday. For the week, that gave him eight homers in six games. According to Mark Gallagher, "Mantle was hitting homers at the greatest rate in American League history. . . . It was the best power spree since Roger Maris hit seven homers in six games in 1961." Gallagher also points out that Mantle's seven homers in five games would have duplicated a record set by Babe Ruth and two others except that Mickey didn't connect in *each* of those first five games. He was homerless in that Boston

Mickey Mantle and Roger Maris pose after both had homered in a game in 1961, the year Maris broke Babe Ruth's single-season record for homers. After 1964 the home run production of Mantle and Maris declined, and Maris was traded to the Cardinals following the 1966 season. [AP/Wide World Photos]

game when the Red Sox hurlers avoided him. Winning is all that counts, right?

It was a cause for joy, of course, but concern as well. What worried me was that Mantle pulled only one of those home runs during that streak, and that shot came on a changeup. Eleven of the other round-trippers were hit to center field or the opposite way. I was happy with the results but was afraid Mickey couldn't get around on the fastball the way he used to. Mantle had never been a strict pull hitter like Maris or Pepitone, but he would pull his homers more often than one out of every eight times. I feared his hot hitting would end if everything about his swing weren't just right. Viewed from today, it shows how smart a hitter Mantle was to be going the other way late in his career.

Mantle's streak ended after that Washington series. The Yankees came back to town, and Mickey's bat turned cold. It sparked up again about five games into the home stand when he hit a homer against Boston and two more against the Senators. It gave him a total of eleven homers in fourteen games, all coming against the Red Sox and Senators. It gave him eighteen four-baggers going into the All-Star break, putting him among the league leaders. All the signs pointed to a comeback season for the Mick.

It was not to be. Riddled with injuries during the second half of the season, Mantle managed only five homers the rest of the way, including a dramatic pinch-hit blast that won a ball game against Detroit. Mickey had been out two weeks with a pulled muscle and was making his first plate appearance since the time of his injury. I wondered if he could duplicate what he had done a few years earlier, when he hit a home run as a pinch-hitter after missing two months of the season. Sure enough, he did.

Mick's injuries were something his fans had to put up with. It was painful watching him run the bases or attempting to steal, fearing he would injure himself. A few years ago, NBC sportscaster Bob Costas asked Mantle to comment on Jose Canseco's hitting forty homers and stealing forty bases. "If I'd have known that was such a big deal," Mantle replied, "I'd have done it every year." He went on to add that he'd have been crazy to try stealing a lot of bases with the kind of hitters they had on those Yankee ball clubs.

Those who saw Mantle play in his early days say he was one of the fastest runners, and he probably could have stolen a lot more bases than he did. But maybe it's better he didn't. Fans don't go to the ball park to see grown men sprinting from first to second. They want to see the ball knocked over the fence. Mickey would steal a base to help win a ball game, not help himself get into the record books.

Playing in a little more than 100 games, Mantle finished the 1966 season batting .288, hitting 23 homers, and driving in 56 runs. Those statistics are impressive enough when you consider that Mickey played on a last-place ball club and opposing pitchers avoided throwing strikes to him. But if you project his stats over the course of 162 games, you realize that Mantle had an excellent year. He would have finished with 34 homers, 84 RBIs, close to 90 walks, 207 total bases, and 140 hits. Fans won't remember it as one of his best seasons; but, taking into account his injuries and lack of support from his teammates, a case could be made that it was.

Nineteen sixty-seven proved to be a similar year for the Mick statistically. He accumulated 191 total bases, scored 63 runs, and made 108 hits. He drew an incredible 170 walks, proving that pitchers around the league still respected what he could do with his bat. He batted .245, however, the lowest in his career except for his last year, and his home run (22) and RBI (55) production, which were about the same as in 1966, came with more than 100 more at bats. Most of his homers came in the first half of the season, as he hit 16 by the All-Star break.

The injuries Mickey suffered that year were minimal, probably due to Ralph Houk's using him at first base. The strategy worked, with Mickey playing in almost forty more games than in 1966. Had Mantle been forced to continue playing in the outfield, he probably would have retired before the season was half over. Instead, he was able to play regularly for another two seasons. It's with good reason that Houk is known for being a player's manager, and because of the way he handled the Mick toward the end of his career and Bobby Murcer at the beginning of his, he's my favorite Yankee manager, past or present.

Although 1967 was a mediocre year for the Yanks and Mantle, it probably was one of the most memorable for Mickey and his admirers. This was the season in which he hit his 500th career home run. I was listening to the game when he connected for number 499 against the Twins. It came on his first at bat of the game, and even though the Yanks were playing on the road, I was rooting for Mickey to hit number 500 and get it over with. I felt that if he didn't do it right away, the pressure would build up and negatively affect his performance. Mickey didn't hit it that day, and my fears proved to be well-founded. He started pressing and slumping with the bat. The rest of the team seemed to be affected as well.

Mickey didn't come through until after another ten games. The Yankees were playing the World Champion Orioles in a doubleheader at the Stadium. It was late in the game, and the Yankees were ahead by a run. Relief ace Stu Miller was on the mound for Baltimore, trying to keep his team close so that they could rally and win, something they did frequently against the Yankees in the late sixties. Miller's being in the game was a good omen because he threw a lot of off-speed pitches. Mantle was having trouble hitting fastballs at that time, and he had always been a good changeup hitter. Miller seemed like the kind of pitcher he could handle. That turned out to be true.

After waiting so long, Mickey was to make me wait no longer. Here's how announcer Jerry Coleman called it:

"Here's the payoff pitch to Mantle . . . (he connects) . . . This is it! There it goes! It's outta here!"

Like any other great television broadcaster, Coleman just let the picture do the talking for the next minute or so.

And what memories fans have of what they witnessed. Mickey wiping his right hand against his pants before taking his final practice swing; his body filling his uniform like no other player; the pitch coming to the plate toward the outside corner; Mantle waiting for what must have seemed to him like an eternity before the ball reached striking distance; Mickey swinging, muscles bulging, and pulling it well into the seats in right; the fans screaming and waving their hands in celebration, with no one still in his seat; Mantle approaching third base in the middle of his home run trot, getting a congratulatory remark from Oriole third baseman Brooks Robinson; Mickey rounding third and getting a rare handshake and slap on the back from third base coach Frank Crosetti; and finally reaching home plate and being congratulated by the next Yankee batter, Elston Howard. The fans continued to go crazy, even after Mickey was in the dugout, hoping he would come

Mantle watches his 500th home run sail into the right-field seats at Yankee Stadium on May 14, 1967. He is currently ranked eighth on the all-time home run list.
[*AP/Wide World Photos*]

out and give them a salute with his cap. He didn't. Ball players in those days didn't showboat like they do today.

As mentioned, Ellie Howard was the first player to congratulate Mantle after he touched home plate. Howard was traded later that year, but it was good that a veteran Yankee like Ellie was still around to be the first to shake the Mick's hand after that home run. Howard was a ball player with class.

Stu Miller later claimed that if Mickey hadn't swung, it would have been ball four, but he was wrong. The ball Mantle hit was definitely a strike on the outside corner of the plate. Ball or strike, he hit it. In Art Rust Jr.'s book, *Legends*, Mickey hints that the shot he hit off Barney Shultz to win game three of the 1964 World Series was his most thrilling. That homer was memorable and exciting for me as well. Mickey's number 500, however, was the most exciting moment in sports that I have ever witnessed.

The fact that almost two weeks had passed since he had hit his 499th might have had something to do with how climactic the homer was. That it came late in his career, at a time when Mickey was providing fans with fewer thrills, probably made me savor the moment even more. Most important, it was the athlete who did it. For about ten years, Mantle had been my hero. Number five hundred was the culmination of all Mickey had accomplished since I began following his career at the age of seven. No other sporting feat could be as significant to me.

One other Mantle homer that year was memorable. He hit it a couple of months after his 500th during a night game against the Minnesota Twins that was televised from Yankee Stadium. The game featured a great pitching duel between Jim Kaat and Al Downing. Minnesota led 1–0 in the bottom of the ninth on a Killebrew round-tripper.

Kaat retired the first two Yanks rather easily, which brought up the Mick. Kaat threw. Ball one. Kaat fired again. Ball two. The next pitch was a strike, followed by ball three. With one out remaining and a one-run lead, I didn't think Kaat would challenge Mickey on a 3–1 pitch. My mistake in thinking was not as great as Kaat's error in judgment. When Mickey swung, I stood frozen. He hit it hard, but to the wrong part of the ball park—Death Valley in left-center field—the part of the stadium that devours home run balls. The ball kept carrying and carrying, and the left fielder kept running farther and farther back. Finally the ball landed in the left-center-field bleachers some four hundred fifty feet away.

It was as if the thunderbolt unleashed by Mantle had opened up the skies. Ellie Howard made the final out of the inning, and the rains came. The game was called and replayed later in the season. In his autobiography, *The Mick,* Mantle relates how devastating his homer was to the Twins that year:

"The Twins lost [the makeup game]. We were in seventh place at the time, but they'd been battling like mad for the pennant, so Kaat's home run pitch really hurt them. They might have won by pitching around me."

Kaat made the decision to challenge Mickey, and he should be respected for it. He was a great pitcher who won nearly three hundred games. More importantly, Kaat always had class. Had Mantle made an out, no one would have thought twice about Kaat's decision and would have lauded his superb shutout pitching. It would have been easy for Jim to throw ball four and go after Ellie. Even if Howard and the Yanks had come through, no one would have faulted Kaat for putting Mantle on. Maybe Jim felt as I do. There's more to baseball than just winning and losing.

Nineteen sixty-eight was Mickey's final year. He tried to continue the following season, but his body wouldn't let him. Mickey relates in *The Mick* how he became convinced:

"I went down to Ft. Lauderdale a few days ahead of the regulars and tried to work out—just a little running—but I couldn't do it. I was convinced. There was no putting off my retirement."

If the designated-hitter rule had been in effect before Mantle retired, Mick might have considered playing an extra season or two freed from the worry of playing defense. There are baseball fans and professionals who are against the use of the designated hitter, but I'm not one of them. I would have given anything to see No. 7 hitting for one more season. American League fans will still enjoy seeing Jose Canseco playing a decade from now when his legs or back become too sore to allow him to play the outfield. When National Leaguer Ryne Sandberg reaches that same stage in his career, he'll be forced to retire or switch leagues. How happy will that make the Windy City residents? Besides, watching pitchers hit is boring. Let's face it, with more offense comes more excitement, which is why soccer will never replace baseball as our national pastime.

Mantle's last season was a poor one. He hit eighteen homers, only the third time in his career that he hit fewer than twenty. More significantly, he batted .237 which, sadly, lowered his lifetime batting average below .300. If he had to do it over again, would Mickey have retired before that 1968 season? True, it would have left Mantle with a lifetime average of .302, but it would not have enabled him to surpass Ted Williams and Jimmy Foxx on the all-time home run list. Fans would have been robbed of another memorable round-tripper as well.

It came against Detroit at Tiger Stadium. Denny McLain had already won thirty games and was well on his way to winning thirty-one. Late in the game, with his team ahead by five runs, McLain faced Mantle. Denny threw a couple of pitches, and suddenly Phil Rizzuto, who was calling the game on radio, got excited. It appeared to him that McLain was throwing some fat pitches for Mickey to hit. When Denny threw the next one, it confirmed what Rizzuto had been saying. The ball landed in the upper deck in right field. The homer, number five hun-

Mantle waves to the crowd during a celebration at Yankee Stadium. The slugger was honored for having hit his 500th homer a few days earlier. Yankee president Mike Burke presides. [Photo by Barton Silverman/New York Times]

dred thirty-five for the Mick, was the next to last of his career. It put him in third place on the home run list at the time, passing the legendary Jimmy Foxx.

In the papers the next day, McLain didn't openly admit to what had taken place, but it was obvious to all who had watched that the four-bagger was a gift from a thirty-game, Cy Young award winner to a legend who would soon be leaving the game. Mick was McLain's idol, he was to say later, and Denny wanted to salute him the best way he knew. And it delighted the crowd with another Mantle memory that will never be forgotten.

I remember that homer today, however, with mixed emotions. McLain was a tough pitcher for an aging Mantle to handle, and without his help Mickey probably wouldn't have hit the homer. But the thought that it was tainted persists. It is aggravated by the fact that it was such a noteworthy round-tripper and that Mickey's next, and last, homer would have enabled him to surpass Foxx anyway. Mick still had to hit it out, of course, not an easy task for any ball player under any circumstances, even during batting practice. It's something he had done five hundred thirty-four times previously, though, off pitchers who hadn't given him any gifts or avoided pitching to him. Kaat had given Mantle a fair chance to hit one out the previous year, and when Mickey did, everyone knew he earned it. What Denny did was a nice gesture, but not classy.

There are three noteworthy aspects of Mickey's final blow. One is that when baseball fans ask who served up Mickey's last home run, the answer will be Jim Lonborg, a notable pitcher who had won the Cy Young award the previous year. Another is that it came in Yankee Stadium, that great ball park where such immortals as Ruth, Gehrig, and Dimaggio had put on a show for forty years before Mantle took over. Finally, I'm glad I was listening to the game that night. For Mantle to have hit his last home run without me watching or listening would have left a void in my following of his career.

Some sportswriters and commentators refer to Mantle as a great ball player, but not quite in the same class as certain past performers. They mention his lifetime batting average being below .300 and that his RBI production was lower than what it should have been after playing on such great teams. They claim also that the number of great years that Mickey put together was fewer than such superstars as Babe Ruth, Lou Gehrig, Willie Mays, Joe Dimaggio, and Ted Williams.

I won't dispute their arguments. There are other qualified sportswriters who have done research on the subject and written their results objectively for readers to make up their own minds. Mark Gallagher's *Explosion* is an example of a book that offers a good comparative study. Admittedly, Gallagher is a Mantle fan, but his book lays out the facts in a fair and detailed manner. Mantle compares favorably with any ball player, past or present, but let some say that he wasn't the greatest. History will show that he was the most popular.

It's interesting that Mick's popularity was at its zenith during the twilight of his career. Perhaps to fans who followed the beleaguered Yankees then, Mantle served as a link to the glorious teams of the past. Maybe watching Mickey struggle with the bat or limp around the bases made us appreciate the greatness that once was his. It could simply be the way he conducted himself on the field, with the quiet leadership and presence that commanded the respect of all his peers and drew our admiration.

For whatever the reason, in Mickey's last four years, he was more popular than any player before or since. The standing ovations he received constantly were not limited to his own ball park either. With the Yankees no longer a threat to win the pennant, fans around the league turned their attention from booing the Yanks to cheering the Mick whenever the team came to town. Even ball players were affected, McLain's free toss in 1968 being a dramatic example.

They realized that Mantle wouldn't be around for long and that when he left baseball, the greatest of our national pastimes, no one like him would emerge.

Mickey seems to be doing well financially these days. He has a successful restaurant in New York, and he appears frequently at baseball card shows, being paid handsomely for signed autographs. Some sportswriters take exception to Mick's making money for what they think are overpriced signatures. One article in a Staten Island paper some time ago criticized Mantle for that very reason and infuriated me to the point of sending in a rebuttal. The paper handled it fairly, printing my letter in article form in the following Sunday edition, along with a blown-up picture of Mickey and Ralph Houk taken at the time of Mantle signing his first $100,000-a-year contract. Here's a part of what I wrote:

> I'm glad the Mick is making money now— finally. He's only making the money off the field that he deserved to be making when he was on the field. If I'm looking to knock ball players, I usually direct my criticism to those still playing the game who are making ten times as much money in a year as Mantle did in any year, and at the same time perform with one tenth the skills and effort that he did.
>
> Although I still revere the Mick as a god, I don't forget that he's only human. I don't forget that, like me, he has a family he loves and cares about and that providing as best he can for himself and his family is nothing to be ashamed about. On the contrary, I have even more respect for him, if that's possible. Rather than worrying about tarnishing his legendary status by conducting himself in a manner that his public admirers deem proper, Mickey is making as much

money as he can, without hurting anyone in the process.

Is that so shameful? It seems to be only sportswriters and commentators who are bemoaning the poor autograph seekers for paying exorbitant prices for superstar signatures. The fans themselves are walking away happy to have met their heroes, however briefly.

How much are all the memories of Mickey Mantle worth? A lot more than the Mick is getting paid for signing autographs. More still than the highest paid superstars are getting paid. If you could sell the memory of Mickey Mantle hitting his five hundredth career home run off of Stu Miller, how much would you ask for? Or what about the one when he hit the five-hundred-foot shot into the dead-centerfield bleachers? How much is that piece of memory worth? And the time when he came off the bench to bat for the first time in two months and hit a homer to gain yet another Yankee victory? Isn't that one worth a couple of hundred thousand?

Fortunately for us, ball players can't ask us to pay for all the memories they have given us while we were kids growing up, searching for heroes to idolize and imitate. Let's not begrudge them the opportunity to sell their autographs. No one's twisting our arms to buy them.

So sportswriters should think of other athletes to pick on when they're in a nasty mood. Mickey Mantle owes us fans nothing and has already given us plenty. Let's be happy when we hear about him making a few bucks by signing autographs or making guest appearances. I really love the Mick, so I am.

(Staten Island Advance, June 10, 1990)

Thanks for the memories, Mick!

CHAPTER TWO

BOBBY MURCER

An All-Star in His Own Right

There's a long drive to right field! If it's fair, it's a home run! It's right down the line! It's a fair ball! It hit the foul pole! Bobby Murcer has hit his fourth home run in a row and third in this ball game!

THAT WAS THE CALL MADE BY YANKEE radio announcer Bob Gamere on the day Bobby Murcer became one of only a score of ball players in major league history to hit four home runs in four consecutive at bats. (Bo Jackson was the most recent player to do it.) It's a feat no other Yankee has duplicated since, and one which many past Yankee superstars were never able to accomplish including Ruth, Dimaggio, Maris, and Reggie Jackson. Marv Albert replayed Gamere's call on his Yankee pregame show the following evening along with Frank Messer's broadcast of Murcer's third shot:

Bobby Murcer [*National Baseball Library, Cooperstown, New York*]

Murcer hits one deep to right! Foster [Indian right fielder] goes back and . . . good golly Miss Molly, Murcer's done it again!

I listened to Albert's show because I wanted to hear the home run calls. I had missed the play-by-play the previous day because I had been at the Stadium when Murcer performed the magic with his wand of wood. It was the most excitement I had ever experienced at the ball park.

It was June 24, 1970. The Yanks were at home playing two games that day. In the first game, Sam McDowell was stifling the Bombers with fastballs. Here was a pitcher who had struck out more than 300 batters in 1965 and would repeat the feat that year. Yet, in the years that followed, Sudden Sam suddenly lost his fastball.

The game was boring for Yankee fans. Steve Hamilton livened things up when Houk brought him in to relieve. Hamilton had begun throwing his lob pitch earlier that year, calling it the "Folly Floater." It was great. The fans loved it, and the pitch was actually effective, fooling batters time after time with its slow approach to the plate. When the Indians' Tony Horton made out on a weak pop-up to the catcher, the fans went wild as Horton, a showman, crawled back to the dugout, feinting agony and disgrace at having missed the meatball thrown to him. The Indians were safely ahead, so the performances by Hamilton and Horton were a pleasant diversion from the ho-hum game Yankee fans were witnessing. But there was much excitement to come.

By the ninth, McDowell was leading 7–1, when Murcer stepped up to the plate. He hadn't done much better with the bat than his teammates to that point, having struck out and popped out twice off the big lefthander. With the count 0–1, Murcer golfed the next pitch well into the seats in straightaway right field.

Even with the Yankee defeat in the opener, there was something to cheer about. It was an especially satisfying home run for a couple of reasons. He hit it off of McDowell, a tough southpaw for lefties, even in his later years. (Throughout his career, Murcer often complained about having to face too many lefty pitchers. When he was going strong, though, Bobby could handle lefties and righties with equal effectiveness.) Secondly, Murcer had been struggling with the bat for the past couple of weeks. Hitting a homer had gotten Bobby out of slumps in the past, and perhaps it would again. But I was surprised that it happened so quickly and in such spectacular fashion.

Bobby resumed his assault by launching one into the right-field seats off Cleveland southpaw Mike Paul in the nightcap. It came in the opening inning, and he duplicated that shot with another in the fifth, again off starter Paul. That made it three homers in three official at bats (he was walked in the third inning), all coming off lefty throwers. For a guy who didn't like to face them, Murcer was doing a good job.

Murcer's third round-tripper was especially sweet, coming after a bench-clearing incident in the top half of the inning. The Indians had a runner on third with two outs. Yankee starter Stan Bahnsen threw a wild one that catcher Thurman Munson couldn't handle cleanly. The Indians' Vada Pinson tried to score, but Thurman scrambled after the ball and fired to Bahnsen covering at the plate. They had him rather easily. Suddenly, Pinson decked Bahnsen with a punch as effective as anything Stan threw that day. Bahnsen wound up on his rear end and was immediately surrounded by Indians. The Yankees rushed to help him and, after the commotion settled, Pinson was thrown out of the game by ump Ron Luciano. That set off another battle, with Tribe manager Al Dark wondering why Bahnsen wasn't sent to the showers along with his rival combatant.

"Pinson threw the first punch," Luciano told reporters after the game.

"Is throwing the first punch automatic ejection?" a reporter asked.

"It is with me," Luciano retorted in typical Luciano style.

Murcer's homer in the fifth was a two-run shot. It gave the Yankees a 3–2 lead and eased my disappointment over the Yankees' loss in the opener. The Indians' Graig Nettles spoiled things, though, with a two-run homer in the eighth, putting Cleveland ahead once again.

It was depressing. Here was a year in which the Bombers were disguising themselves as contenders. It was late June, and they trailed the first-place Orioles by only three games. I was optimistic that the Yankees would grab their first pennant in six years. A second loss in the nightcap would be tragic.

When the game moved to the bottom of the eighth, there wasn't much cause for hope. Although a formidable team that year, the Yankees rarely produced come-from-behind victories; and the way they were swinging the bats that day, I was even more convinced that it wouldn't happen. Murcer was due to bat second in the inning, but I couldn't count on another long ball from him. He had hit three already, and the last Yankee to hit four consecutive home runs was Mickey Mantle. Murcer was no Mantle, no matter how hard the Yankee brass tried to make the fans believe it.

Fred Lasher was pitching in relief for the Indians and promptly retired Horace Clarke on a ground ball. That brought up Bobby, who batted second in the batting order in those days. The count went to 3–2. The next day, two papers reported that Murcer fouled off seven pitches, three of them coming on a full count. Watching from the stands, it seemed more like twenty. Murcer then hit one deep down the line in right. There were 32,000 at the Stadium that day and surely they all rose to their feet, peering from whatever position they were in, leaning with body English to the fair side of the foul pole. I didn't see the ball hit the pole, but I'll take Gamere's word for it. I cheered and applauded as Bobby performed his home run trot for the fourth time. (No one could do a home run trot like Mickey Mantle, but Bobby had a good one.) He touched home plate, shook hands with Roy White, and lifted his cap high in the air, saluting the crowd. As he approached the dugout, Ralph Houk was the first to congratulate him. The crowd kept cheering, but Murcer never came out for a curtain call.

The Yankees scored another run that inning and went on to win, but I didn't care. I had witnessed something that millions of people attending baseball games in the past never had. That was more important. The Yankees would finish in second place, a sizable distance behind Baltimore, but it didn't take away the memory of what Murcer did that day.

Incredibly, it was not the first time Murcer had hit four consecutive round-trippers. "Would you believe I hit four in a row at Toledo?" Murcer told reporters after the game. "I did it in the same way. I hit a homer the last time up the first game, then three in a row the second. This was a lot more fun."

Nor was it the last time Bobby would hit three homers in one game. I saw him do it on television one night, and although it didn't match the excitement of that four-homer day at Yankee Stadium, it was still a thrill.

The date was July 13, 1973, almost precisely three years after his first triple-homer Major League game. The Yanks were playing Kansas City on a Friday night—Friday the 13th. Gene Garber, a sidearm-throwing righthander, was pitching for the Royals, and Murcer didn't waste much time putting the Yanks in front with a three-run clout in the opening frame. After making an out in the third, Bobby reached the seats in the sixth, again off Garber. When he came up for his final try in the eighth inning, the fans greeted him with cheers and shouts of encouragement, as if sending the message, "Hey friend, do it again!" The screams were silenced abruptly as Garber, still in the game for the Royals, sent his own message, hurling the ball over Bobby's head on the first pitch.

"I expected to be dusted," Murcer said after the game. "It just made me more determined to hit another one."

That is exactly what he did, driving the next pitch into the right-field bullpen. When Bobby took his time rounding the bases, Garber became perturbed. "The man showed me up," he complained afterward. "He didn't have to do that!"

After the 5–0 win, the reporters had some fun with Murcer, reminding him of his first three-homer game and that doing it twice was something Mantle was never able to do.

"Oh no, don't start that stuff again!" Bobby cried. "I thought that was buried for all time! I've never considered myself a home run hitter. You have to be lucky to hit three in one game."

Houk joined in the teasing, claiming that he signed Bobby for considerably less than he had intended to pay. Murcer retorted, "I could have gotten more from the Dodgers, but I wanted to sign with the Yankees because they played in the World Series every year." As it turned out, Bobby never played in the series as a Yankee regular.

It's interesting to note that Murcer's two big days came during the seasons when he had his lowest home run totals playing as a regular at the Stadium. That personifies the kind of hitter he was—streaky at times, slumping at others. After his explosion against Garber, Bobby wouldn't hit another home run for another five weeks, when he finally connected off Sonny Siebert of Texas.

"When I hit three home runs, I told you guys I wasn't a home run hitter," Murcer reminded reporters. "Usually when I hit a home run, I get back into a groove. Maybe I'm ready to get a hot streak going." It didn't turn out that way. Bobby hit only three more the rest of the year. One of them—off Gaylord Perry— was probably as satisfying to Murcer as the three he hit against Garber.

Most of Murcer's troubles throughout his career came from facing tough lefthanders, but his biggest nemesis was right-handed spitball throwing Perry. Murcer never hid the fact that he didn't like Gaylord's moistening the ball once in a while. After flustering Bobby game after game, Perry, with tongue in cheek, would always claim his innocence of any wrongdoing when talking to reporters.

No one complained about Gaylord's alleged

tricks as often or as vociferously as Bobby. Early in 1972 Perry shut out the Yanks at the Stadium and dealt Murcer a usual zero for four. Reporters went to home plate umpire John Rice afterward and asked if he had any suspicions of Perry's wrongdoings during the game. "No one said a word until the last hitter, Murcer," claimed Rice. "He started beefing on every pitch, but I didn't see anything that looked funny. Perry throws the ball over the plate, has something on it, and moves it around. He hasn't got me too suspicious." You couldn't convince Bobby.

Later that same year, Murcer experienced his first success in a game against Perry, getting two hits and lining out in four at bats. Later Bobby talked with new confidence to reporters about his ability to hit against the crafty veteran. "I just decided to keep swinging and stop talking and see what happened," he explained. "This time I managed to hit a couple, and I'm determined to hit a homer off him in the Stadium."

Sure enough, it finally happened, but it didn't come until the following year on what turned out to be Murcer's last crack at Perry at the Stadium. (The next year the Yanks played at Shea, and Murcer was traded at the end of that season.) Murcer's revenge came in a losing cause, and there wasn't much of a write-up in the papers the next day. But I'm sure Bobby enjoyed his home run trot that day as much as he did following the blast against Garber.

My interest in Murcer's career began in 1969 in his first season as a Yankee regular. In the opening game of the year, Murcer and rookie Jerry Kenney blasted home runs to help the Yankees win, 8–4, in Washington. "I was glad to see Bobby and Jerry get off good to help their confidence," Houk commented after the game." It may have helped Murcer, but Kenney's career didn't last long. His fielding and hitting didn't develop as well as the Yanks had hoped it would.

In the home opener the following week, Bobby hit an upper deck shot that opened some eyes. The sports headline of a Staten Island paper the next day read, "Murcer—Yankee Fans New Hero."

"I've been waiting a long time to hit one at the Stadium," Murcer said after the game. "I haven't played many games here [he played a few in 1966 before fulfilling military obligations the next two years] and never came close to a homer. Now I have broken the ice." When Murcer had his first two-homer game against the Indians later that month, he became my new hero, too.

Bobby began the year playing third base, but his fielding was atrocious. Too often he would misplay ground balls or, even more frequently, make errant throws. Houk would have been justified in pulling him out of the lineup, even though Bobby was swinging the hottest bat on the Yankees for the first two months. Instead, the wise manager decided to try Murcer at a new position—right field. "I don't know if this will work out or not, but I can't wait any longer to make moves," a worried Houk told reporters in May 1969. "Murcer has been having it tough at third base, and I can't let him destroy himself thinking about it. He's too good a ball player to hurt, so we'll try this." No wonder Houk was Bobby's favorite manager.

After moving to right field, Murcer never returned to the infield. Later, he became the Yankees' center fielder and remained there throughout Houk's tenure as manager, moving back to right field under new skipper Bill Virdon in 1974. With Murcer in the outfield, Kenney was brought in from center and forced to take over at third base. He did little better than Murcer with his hop-skip-throw routine, but Bobby was doing too well with his bat and glove for Houk to fool around with positions again. Ralph's brilliant move didn't help Kenney's career, but it saved Bobby's and helped pave his way to stardom.

Murcer responded to the move immediately by hitting a home run in his first game as a right fielder. It came against the Seattle Pilots. That game was significant, not because of the position switch, but because it came after a Yankee–Pilot brawl the day before, a brawl initiated by Murcer himself. The round-tripper was sweet revenge for Bobby, although the Yankees eventually lost the contest.

In the first game of the series, Murcer connected off Pilot starter Marty Pattin for a two-run homer. In his next at bat, Bobby had to duck under a fastball heading toward his eyes. Murcer didn't charge the mound, the fashionable thing to do in later years. Instead, he promptly lined a hit to right and hustled toward second base. When the throw to shortstop Ray Oyler arrived ahead of him, Bobby charged into second none too gently. Oyler and the ball went flying, and soon Murcer was covered with Pilots. The first Yankee to join the festivities was Houk, who promptly dove into the melee. Immediately, Pilot players came flying out. "I was trying to get down to where they had Bobby buried. I'd rather be hurt than see him injured," Houk bellowed to reporters afterward. "If they want to play like that, they'll get a shock. Just because a kid hits a homer, there's no cause to throw at his head the next time up." It was Murcer's first and only fight in his Major League career. Maybe opposing clubs heard the Major's words of warning.

At the end of the month, Murcer won a ball game with a two-run double in the ninth, beating Rudy May and the Angels 2–1. Going into the last inning, the Yankees had only managed a Horace Clarke single, but Bill Robinson and Tresh kept things alive with back-to-back hits. With two outs, Murcer lined a fastball off the tough lefthander that landed just inside the right-field line, and the game was over. Murcer was red hot. In his first full season, he was leading the majors with thirty-eight RBI's after two months.

Unfortunately, Bobby's bat was to cool off quite a bit. He hurt himself in a freak play against Kansas City in June and wound up missing half a dozen games. When he returned to the lineup, he forgot to bring his hot bat with him, and his average plummeted. His home run and RBI production trailed off as well, and Bobby began pressing. After striking out five times in a doubleheader against Detroit, he complained to reporters, "I don't know why I'm not hitting. I'm missing pitches I should be hitting out of the park. . . . I'm not seeing the ball good when I try to bunt." Murcer was in his first of several slumps that would plague him throughout his career. He would prove to be a star, but just as Mantle had been frustrated at the plate for lengthy periods of time during his playing days, including his first full season, so too would Bobby. Like Mickey though, when Murcer was hot, few were his equal.

As he often did, Murcer came out of his slump in dramatic and spectacular fashion. It happened in a game in early August against California at Yankee Stadium. The Yanks went into the last frame trailing 2–0. With two outs, Ron Woods and Frank Fernandez reached base on walks, which brought up Murcer. Angel manager Lefty Phillips yanked hurler Ken

Tatum in favor of lefty Clyde Wright. Bobby didn't waste any time, socking Wright's first pitch into the right-field seats. It was his first homer in Yankee Stadium since mid-April and only his third in six weeks. It was a different Bobby Murcer who talked to the press after the game. "I knew if Frank got on they would bring in a lefthander. I'm glad Ralph let me hit," beamed Bobby. "Man, what a feeling to finally do something. I haven't had much to smile about lately. Maybe this is the night my luck will change."

Ball players are often superstitious. Maybe bad fortune had been following Murcer around, causing his batting woes. Perhaps a lack of confidence in his hitting ability, causing Bobby to think too much at the plate, is a more logical explanation. Whatever the cause, his game-winning homer became the cure. Murcer's hot bat returned with a vengeance.

In the next game, Murcer picked on the Angels again, connecting for three hits, including his fifteenth homer in the ninth inning off knuckleballer Hoyt Wilhelm, leading the Yanks to a 3–1 win. He went on to hit eight homers in August. Bobby had the biggest day of his young career the following month, walloping three home runs in a double-header against the Boston Red Sox.

All things considered, Bobby had an impressive first year, hitting twenty-six homers, more than most superstars of the past had accomplished in their rookie years, including Gehrig, Mays, Mantle, and Berra. Murcer had done enough to keep alive my interest in his career and in the Yankees, who lost the pennant for the fifth straight season.

Bobby's best year was 1972, but it started out poorly. His performance for the first two months was an antithesis of April and May 1969. He had only one home run, and his batting average (.331 the year before) and RBI production were low.

Then came a game in early June against Milwaukee that became the turning point of the season for Bobby. The Yanks were on the road, and Murcer got them off to a good start, doubling in a run in the first inning to give the Bombers a 1–0 lead. It didn't last long, as Milwaukee scored three in the second and another three in the sixth. The Yanks came from behind nicely, but were still one run short by the ninth inning. Murcer came up with one out and belted a 1–1 pitch deep into the right-field seats. It gave him a total of four hits for the game, and he was robbed of two others by George Scott, always nifty with the leather at first base. The Yanks lost in twelve innings, but after the game the Yankee announcers looked for some bright spots in a tough Yankee loss. They pointed out that Murcer's quadruple-hit game could awaken him from the deep sleep he had been experiencing at the plate.

They were right. The game marked the beginning of a torrid June and the end of his slump. After homering off Kansas City's Dick Drago in the middle of the month, an elated Murcer said, "I told you before we started that last trip [which began in Milwaukee] that I was ready to go. I just had the feeling. How do I know when I've got it? When they can't throw a fastball past me or fool me with a change when they have two strikes on me. I'm on every pitch."

He would be on a lot more pitches before the month ended. When Bobby hit a four-bagger against Tiger southpaw Mickey Lolich in late June, it gave him eight homers, twenty-one RBIs, and a .391 batting average for the month, launching him toward the biggest home run and RBI season of his career.

Murcer stayed red-hot in July, hitting eight more homers that month during a fourteen-game hitting streak that raised his average over .290 for the season. His success didn't come from facing easy pitchers either. I recall watching Old-Timers' Day on television that year when the Yanks were playing two against California. The Bombers lost 1–0 in eleven innings in the first game and were facing strikeout leader Nolan Ryan in the second. Ryan was having a good year with an 11–8 record and a low ERA. Murcer put the Yanks on the scoreboard for the first time that day, walloping a Ryan fastball for a home run. In the next inning, Bobby picked on another Ryan heater, roping it down the line for a double. When Murcer was hot, it was difficult for any pitcher to get him out.

Murcer did everything that year. During one game in early August he was called on to pinch-hit against the Red Sox in Boston late in the game. He went the opposite way and knocked the ball over the left-field wall. Bobby rarely hit with power to left, but he wisely took advantage of the short distance to the wall whenever he played at Fenway. "It was the first homer I ever hit into the left-field screen," he told reporters later. "I've hit the wall before, but never the screen."

It wasn't his first pinch-homer, however. Said Murcer, "I hit a pinch-homer before. In fact it was a grand slam, off Lew Krausse in Milwaukee." Talking about that bases-loaded round-tripper might have gotten Bobby to thinking that it was time to do it again. Two days later he hit the second one of his career, by coincidence against Milwaukee.

Murcer hit seven more home runs in August, including two in a doubleheader against the Texas Rangers at the end of the month. It also was the first and only time in his career as a Yankee that Murcer hit for the cycle—hitting a home run, double, triple, and single in one game. He did it in the first game, tying it up in the last inning with a home run and eventually enabling the Yanks to win it in eleven innings.

Murcer was more subdued afterward than would be expected considering he had just accomplished a feat that only a small percentage of ball players had ever done. His quiet demeanor was because the Yanks had dropped the second game of the twin bill. "If we had won both games, there would have been a lot of quotes," Murcer sullenly remarked to reporters. "I would have given you a lot of copy . . . all you could handle. It makes a lot of difference if you win."

He did compare the thrill of his accomplishment with another one a couple of years earlier. "This was a good night," he said, "but I'll still take those four homers in a row as a top thrill. After all, it's tough to beat four straight homers like I got two years ago in a doubleheader with Cleveland. This wasn't too bad, but I'll still take the homers."

In the very next game, Murcer treated fans to yet another thrill . . . hitting his one hundredth career home run as a Yankee. As with many of Bobby's homers, it was an important one to the team—the three-run shot giving Fritz Peterson an early, comfortable lead en route to a victory. Of the hundreds of ball players who have played for that great team, Murcer became only the twentieth Yankee to reach the century mark. Again, team player Murcer was talking about what could have been for the club in postgame interviews rather than his milestone home run. "I just regret I got off to such a slow start. Looking back, if I had been able to drive in a few runs earlier in the year, we could be in first place by now."

As mentioned previously, Murcer did it all that year, not only with his bat. Bobby threw numerous base runners out at third and at home. He committed few misplays in the outfield while robbing batters of would-be hits with brilliant catches.

I was at Yankee Stadium for a game in early September, and although Murcer's 0–4 at the plate was disappointing, he showed what he could do with the leather. Murcer made three dazzling plays in the first couple of innings, which turned out to be game-savers as the Yanks won 2–1. In the first inning the White Sox had two men on base when Murcer made a running one-handed catch to prevent a run from scoring. Chicago's first two batters reached base the next inning, but again it was Bobby to the rescue. He made another running catch to rob Luis Alvarado of a hit and with two out did the same to Pat Kelly, this time catching the ball off his shoetops in short center after a long run. The White Sox should have scored at least two runs in the inning, but, thanks to Murcer, they were denied.

The Yanks went on to lose the pennant that year with a swan dive in September, despite Murcer's continued hot hitting. He hit nine home runs during that last month, giving him a total of thirty-three along with ninety-six RBIs at season's end. Considering that the Yanks played ten fewer games during that strike-shortened season, Murcer's stats for 1972 were indeed impressive. It was a year to remember for Bobby, topping even the previous one when he was runner-up for the batting title.

After the 1974 season, Bobby Murcer was traded for Bobby Bonds of San Francisco. Bonds was an outstanding ball player in his own right, and I was anxious to watch him perform in pinstripes. He did not disappoint with his bat, hitting thirty home runs that year, although striking out a lot. He never played another season for the Yankees and was traded at the end of the year.

Although I liked and rooted for Bonds, I was crushed when the Yanks traded Murcer. He had played brilliantly for the ball club each season and was their only legitimate star (Munson was only starting to come into his own). The team, and manager Bill Virdon in particular, seemed to be back-stabbing Bobby by shipping him off to Candlestick. Murcer and Virdon hadn't seemed to get along since the manager moved Bobby to right field in 1974, preferring the speedier Elliot Maddox in center. Bobby hadn't helped his cause much either with all his complaining that year about the effect of the winds at Shea Stadium on his home run production. He pointed to the numerous fly-ball outs he made that would have been four-baggers at Yankee Stadium. Since the club was considering playing one more season at Shea, perhaps Virdon and the Yankees decided Bobby's usefulness to the team had diminished. Never mind that in the six previous seasons he had hit more home runs and had knocked in more runs than any other Yankee. Murcer had an off year, and so it was time for him to go. Such loyalty by the Yankee brass.

When baseball people talk about Murcer's career, they often mention that Bobby was unfairly compared to Mickey Mantle. He came from Oklahoma as did Mantle, was signed by Tom Greenwade, the scout who signed Mickey, and began as a shortstop, Mantle's first fielding position. These experts argue that fan expectations were too high, and it put too much pressure on Murcer. Former Yankee shortstop Tony Kubek once commented, "Bobby could never have lived up to what people expected of him, and when he didn't they came down on him. But he's a good hitter, a good fielder, a good runner, and he's smart."

If there was pressure on Murcer, it didn't affect his performance. If the fans' expectations were high, how disappointed could they have become? Bobby's career was an outstanding one, a fact evident from his statistics.

Murcer played full-time for the Yanks, Giants, and Cubs for ten seasons. During that time, he averaged twenty-one home runs and eighty-seven RBIs per season. He hit at least twenty homers in seven of those ten years and had a career high thirty-three in 1972, second best in the league. He led the American League in runs scored with a career high one hundred two in 1972 and won the Gold Glove for outfielders. Along with his home run and RBI production that year, Murcer would have been a strong candidate for MVP had his team not died out during the stretch run for the pennant in September, winding up six games behind Detroit.

Murcer's lifetime stats are just as impressive. He hit two hundred fifty-two home runs, eighteen fewer than Roger Maris. His lifetime batting average is .277, but during the seasons he played as a regular it was over .280. He was an All-Star for five straight seasons, from 1971 to 1975, the last year as a National League representative. There is no need to defend Murcer; his career statistics speak for themselves. And if he wasn't Mickey Mantle's equal, neither was anyone else.

Murcer had a reputation for being a bit of a whiner, perhaps justifiably so. He complained while a Yankee regular about having to face too many lefties. He complained about Gaylord Perry's illegal wet ones. He complained about being shifted from

Murcer acknowledges the crowd's applause after driving in his 1,000th run on June 4, 1981. [AP/Wide World Photos]

center to right field by Virdon. He complained about the lost home runs at Shea. He complained about the difficulties in fielding and hitting at Candlestick Park when playing for San Francisco. And he complained about playing day games at Wrigley Field as a Cub and the poor fan support he received at Chicago. When you think about it, though, he was right in almost every case.

Murcer was traded back to the Yankees in June 1979, and it was a welcome homecoming for Bobby and Yankee fans alike. "I felt like a visitor playing in those other places," Murcer said upon his return, referring to the years he played at Shea, Candlestick, and Wrigley. A reporter asked him if Yankee Stadium was the best place to play ball. "It's the only place," Bobby replied. When he returned to center field for the first time in five and one-half years in a game against the Red Sox, the crowd cheered loud and long.

Bobby played for the Yankees an additional three and one-half years, finally quitting in the middle of the 1983 season. During that span he delivered quite a few long balls and clutch hits as a part-timer. I remember one game in which he parked a fastball off flamethrower Jim Kern into the upper deck in right field, leading the Yanks to victory. I also recall his last at bat in the 1981 World Series, the only year of his career that he played in the Fall Classic. Trailing in the series by three games to two, the Yankees were playing at the Stadium. Pitcher Tommy John was due up in the fourth inning with the game tied, 1–1. The bases were loaded with two outs when manager Bob Lemon took a gamble and used Murcer as a pinch-hitter. Bobby drove a screaming liner to right that was caught on the warning track. Had he gotten under it just a little, it would have been four runs and probably the game for the Yankees. It would have changed the complexion of the series, and the Yanks might have been able to turn things around. The record books will show only that it was the third out of the inning.

George Frazier was brought in to relieve in the next inning, and the Dodgers jumped on him for some runs and won the game 9–2 and the series. John complained afterward about being taken out for a pinch-hitter so soon in the contest, but bringing Murcer up in that situation was the correct call. It just didn't work out.

For me, the most memorable game Murcer ever played was on August 6, 1979, the day the Yankees attended the funeral of an old friend— Thurman Munson. Munson had died in a tragic plane crash a few days earlier, and players and fans alike were still trying to get over the shock of what had happened. Murcer, who had been a close friend of Thurman's, was asked by Munson's wife to deliver a eulogy at the funeral. With tears rolling down his cheeks, Bobby saluted his fallen teammate, pausing often to control his emotions:

The life of a soul on Earth lasts longer than his departure. He lives on in your life and the life of all others who knew him. . . . Someday the Yankees may have another captain. . . . No greater honor could be bestowed on a man than to be a successor to this man.

He was No. 15 on the field and he will be No. 15 at the doors of Cooperstown. . . . But history will record my friend as No. 1.

*   *   *

Those moving words were only part of the drama that Murcer was to provide on that mournful day. The Yankees played the first-place Orioles that night. It was the ABC Monday night game of the week, but watching the game at home and listening to Al Michaels and Howard Cosell do the play-by-play wasn't enough for my brother Gene and me. Not that night.

We arrived at the Stadium a few minutes before the Yanks took the field. While a moment of silence was observed in memory of Munson, Gene shoved my shoulder and pointed to Reggie Jackson in right field with his hat in hand and his head bowed. Even though I was 400 feet away in the upper deck behind the third base line, I could tell Reggie was sobbing. The Stadium was packed with 35,000 fans, all of whom were caught up in the emotion of the occasion—a final farewell to their hero.

When the game began, the crowd seemed to get into the traditional spirit of a baseball game. Although the Yankees were far behind the Orioles in the standings and had already lost the first two games of the series, we wanted them to win this one. With Ron Guidry on the mound, we thought they had a chance.

However, the Orioles got off to an early start. Murcer misplayed a ball in left field that led to a run, and by the seventh inning, the Yanks were trailing 4–0 against Dennis Martinez, who looked invincible that night. The boo-birds began making themselves heard around the park, proving fans will be fans no matter what the occasion.

It's a miracle that Murcer was able to start the game. The previous night, Lou Piniella and he had stayed up with Thurman's widow, Diane, offering consolation. Murcer insisted on playing. "I know that that's what Thurman would have wanted," he said later. "If he were sitting here and I said I couldn't play, he'd say, 'You're crazy!'" As it turned out, it was a good thing for the Yanks that he did.

Murcer came up in the bottom of the seventh with two men on base and two outs. On a two-strike pitch, Bobby slammed the next delivery into the lower right-field seats. It was his first homer as a Yankee since his return two months earlier. The crowd erupted and kept cheering long after he returned to the dugout. Murcer never came out to acknowledge the cheers. There was more work to do.

The Yanks now trailed 4–3, and the game stayed that way going into the final inning. The Orioles' Dennis Martinez had given way to Tippy Martinez. Bucky Dent led off with a walk. When Willie Randolph attempted a sacrifice, Martinez picked up the ball and threw to the right fielder instead of the second baseman. When the dust settled, the Yankees had the tying run on third and the winning run at second with Murcer due up. The stage was set.

Martinez was about the best reliever in the game that year, and he was almost unhittable by lefty batters. Normally the situation called for a pinch-hitter, but Manager Billy Martin understood the drama unfolding and let Murcer bat. When the count went to 0–2, Gene and I were already looking ahead to Chris Chambliss, the next batter in the lineup. "He's a lefty too," Gene said. "The Yanks are going to have trouble getting the tying run home. Forget about the winning run." Fortunately, Murcer had more confidence in himself than we did. "I just had a feeling he wasn't going to get me out," Bobby said later.

Murcer lined the next pitch the opposite way to left field. It brought both runners home, the Yankees out of the dugout, and the fans out of their seats.

Martin was one of the first to reach Bobby and congratulate him. On his way to the dugout, Murcer raised his cap to the fans, saluting them for the second time in his career. If that day at the Stadium when he hit four consecutive homers was the most thrilling I've ever experienced, then this one had to be the most emotional. I turned from Gene to wipe the tears from my eyes.

The next day, the *Daily News* had a drawing of Bobby swinging a bat, with words next to it praising him for his dramatic heroics. The *New York Times* sports headline read, "Murcer Drives in Five As Yanks Win 5–4," next to a picture of Billy Martin crying at Munson's funeral. A paper on Staten Island had a picture of Bobby lifting his hat to the crowd. Seeing Bobby's eyes looking skyward, it seemed that maybe he was saluting Thurman and not the crowd, saying goodbye to his friend for the last time.

Bobby Murcer was a special ball player for me. With Mantle it had been different. I had grown up revering the Mick, but so did everyone else. He was and still is a legend. His fame will last long after he and I are gone. Murcer left me with memories that are special because, although he was my favorite, he wasn't everyone's. During Bobby's early years, the Mets were the talk of the town. Murcer's heroics were often lost at the bottom of sports pages in newspapers more interested in writing about Tom Seaver, Ron Swoboda, Nolan Ryan, or Willie Mays. For instance, the day after his spectacular four-homer day in 1970, Murcer had to settle for second billing in the *New York Times*. The Mets' sweep of a doubleheader against the Cubs grabbed the headlines.

Bobby never had the national attention either. He didn't play in a league championship or World Series until very late in his career. During his most productive seasons, the Yankees were out of the pennant picture annually. Brooks Robinson, Frank Robinson, Carl Yastrzemski, Willie Horton, and Reggie Jackson were getting most of the national press coverage. It was rare to see the Yanks on the NBC game of the week in those days.

He won't make the Hall of Fame, but I'll remember Bobby Murcer as the best ball player the Yankees had from 1969 to 1974. If they never put a plaque for him in the center-field monument section at Yankee Stadium, it won't matter. He'll still remain special with me.

Thanks for the memories, Bobby!

CHAPTER THREE

JOE PEPITONE

Hot Dog Hero

WITH HIS LONG HAIR AND SIDEBURNS, Joe Pepitone fit right in with the sixties. He was the first to bring a hair dryer into the locker room, and his tight-fitting uniform made the ladies forget about singing heartthrob Tom Jones. He had a carefree, happy-go-lucky attitude that made it difficult for the fans to dislike him. He was the Yankee hot dog hero.

Pepi was to baseball what Joe Namath was to football, but, unlike Namath, Pepitone wasn't a rebel. He was different because that's the way he was. He didn't go out of his way to fight the establishment. On the contrary, Pepi seemed to have an honest respect for authority figures such as his parents, the manager, and veteran teammates. And he loved being a Yankee. If Joe Dimaggio had left and gone away, Joe Pepitone was there to stay.

Pepi loved attention. Where some ball players were shy and avoided the press and others even despised the media, Joe liked talking to reporters. In fact, at times he felt left out when the press would

49

Joe Pepitone [National Baseball Library, Cooperstown, New York]

turn to his teammates instead of him for post-game interviews. After a game in 1969 when the youngster Bobby Murcer was getting all the attention, Pepi kiddingly yelled to reporters, "Please, can't just one of you come over here and ask a question or two?" A few days later, he teased Bobby in the locker room. "C'mon Murcer! I didn't bother you when you were the hero the other day. Get out of here and let me have some fun. You'll be hitting all year. I may not!"

You could never tell what Pepi would say or do next. Once in Detroit, Joe complained to Bruce Henry, the road secretary then, about the cramped quarters he was given at the hotel. "The one they gave me is so small, I can't get my hair dryer in with me. I had to walk in sideways or I couldn't make it through." He ended up getting general manager Lee MacPhail's suite. Naturally, that night Pepitone hit a homer, a double, and two singles along with three RBIs, leading the Yankees to a 9–4 rout of the Tigers. "It's all because of the great night I spent in Mac-Phail's suite," Pepi kidded afterward. "I felt so relaxed and enjoyed all the niceties of a big suite that I was inspired to a big effort. Maybe I could hit like that all the time if I had a suite every night."

Pepi even tried singing once. Tom Tresh and he once performed a duet for Phil Rizzuto in the broadcast booth. It must have gone to Joe's head because later that year he appeared on television singing "Around the World." He has a nice voice but I thought, "Pepitone's no Wayne Newton. He better stick to baseball." I don't recall Pepitone making any other singing appearances, so maybe he felt the same way.

At times Pepi could amaze fans and even himself with spectacular hitting and fielding. Unfortunately, he wasn't consistent throughout his career.

After one game in 1969 in which he hit a home run and stole two bases, Pepi remarked, "I know the wise guys say this will last only a little while. I'm going to fool them this time. If this is the way it is when you hustle and bear down all the time, then this is how I want to play. This could turn out to be my best year." As it turned out, it was his most trouble-filled one and his last as a Yankee.

Pepi reminded me of the character Johnny in the Alfred Hitchcock classic *Suspicion*. In the old flick, Johnny, played by Cary Grant, is a devil-may-care individual who can't help being irresponsible. A dashing, worldly playboy, Johnny could have had his pick from scores of beautiful lady admirers. Instead, he marries a shy, conservative local girl (played by Oscar winner Joan Fontaine) because she's different from the others. Jobs never seem to last with Johnny because having a good time is always more important. Frustrated, Johnny's wife decides to leave him but changes her mind. She just can't get herself to hate lovable Johnny.

It was the same with Pepitone and the Yankees. His personality often got in the way of his duties with the club. Had he taken baseball more seriously, many will say, Joe could have been a Hall of Famer. But problems arose off the field that affected his performance on it. Finally, in spite of his talent, the organization had to trade him away.

Being traded from the Yankees might have devastated some players (prior to the Steinbrenner reign, that is), but it didn't seem to bother Joe. He boasted that at least he had been traded for a quality ball player, Curt Blefary, and that perhaps a change of scenery was what he needed to keep his mind on the game. Pepi once said that he was thankful to God for being blessed with a great body and for being born

Italian. He would have those qualities wherever he played. Nothing could bring Joe down.

It may be true that Pepitone never reached his full potential, but how can we be sure? Who's to say what a person's true potential is? If we judge Pepi according to standards set by our own personalities, we should let others do the same for us. He would then have a lot of company as an "underachiever."

Pepitone can look back to his career in baseball with pride. He played regularly for the Yankees for seven straight seasons, beginning in 1963 when he hit twenty-seven homers. He followed that with another twenty-eight in 1964, along with a grand slam home run in the World Series. He hit a career high thirty-one in 1966 (winning the Gold Glove award for the second straight year as well), and twenty-seven in his final year as a Yankee. Just as Murcer did well away from the Stadium for a few years, so did Pepitone. He hit twenty-six homers in 1970 playing for the Houston Astros and Chicago Cubs, almost double the number Curt Blefary hit for the Yanks that year. (While playing for the Orioles during the mid-sixties, Blefary had been a Yankee-killer, hitting one ball after another into the lower stands in right field whenever his team played at Yankee Stadium. The Yanks hoped Blefary, playing eighty-one games with the short porch as a target, would have some big years with them. It didn't happen, and Blefary's stay was a short one.) In 1971, Pepi's home run production declined, but he hit .307 playing for the Cubs, the first and only time in his career that he batted over .300. Joe Pepitone's career statistics are fairly impressive, especially for an "underachiever."

My memories of Pepitone's playing days reflect the kind of career he had. He had productive days and streaks when he performed with the qualities of

Pepitone's best season came in 1966. Here Joe is being greeted by Roger Maris after slamming one of his thirty-one round-trippers that year. [Photo by Ernie Sisto/New York Times]

an All-Star. He also had bad times, coming as a result of bad luck, poor effort, or an explosive temper. And there were incidents involving Pepi during games, along with his amusing comments afterward, that made it fun being a fan of Joe Pepitone.

One particular day best typifies Joe's career. The Yankees were playing a doubleheader against the Oakland A's. It was late in the season and both teams were far behind Detroit in the pennant race, but the Bombers were trying to catch the fifth-place A's, who were only three games ahead of them. Pepi won the first game with a home run in the fourth inning, helping Mel Stottlemyre pick up the victory.

In the nightcap, the Yanks were trailing by a run

when Pepitone came up with the tying run on third and one out. He popped up, and the runner was left stranded. Late in the game, Joe had another opportunity to tie the score with a runner on third but again failed. The Yanks eventually knotted the game, forcing extra innings. In the tenth, the A's Mike Hershberger reached base on an infield hit. Reggie Jackson blooped a hit to center field. Pepi, who had been playing in the outfield ever since Mantle was switched to first the previous year, didn't charge the ball the way he should have. Maybe he was thinking about his two futile at bats that cost the Yanks a couple of runs. When Hershberger noticed Pepitone's slowness in reaching the ball, he took off for home and beat Pepi's throw by a whisker. The Yanks were shut down in the bottom of the inning and lost 4–3. Angry at himself, Pepitone did not stay in the clubhouse to face reporters afterward. Instead, Manager Houk met the press and, as always, was quick to defend his ball player. "I don't think Joe saw the ball too good," he commented. "Don't forget, it's a strange light at that time of night and it's a little hard to pick up the ball."

Houk's generous words couldn't hide the fact that Pepi had dogged it. As with his career, Joe had gone through an emotional roller coaster that day, winning one game with his bat and losing one with his lack of concentration.

Sometimes a ball player does something that isn't very important to the team or his career, yet it's something a fan remembers the rest of his life. Two of Pepitone's inconsequential home runs remain the most memorable for me. He hit one of them in a game against the California Angels at Yankee Stadium. The Yanks were losing by a couple of runs when he came up to hit in the ninth. Joe had been complaining about a bruised wrist for about a week; so while Pepi was batting, the camera switched to Jimmy Piersall, who was standing in the California dugout and waving a towel at Pepitone. Piersall wrapped it around his wrist, cringing on his knees in mock agony. He repeated his act several times between pitches, being sure to attract Joe's attention each time.

Pepitone observed Piersall without saying a word. It was shaping up to be the battle of the two hot-dog kings. Both Piersall and Pepitone were well-known for the knack of saying and doing the unusual.

For the comic scene Yankee fans were being treated to that day, Pepi would play his part by first letting his bat do his talking, lining a vicious drive into the right-field seats. Joe took his sweet time touching the bases, and as he rounded third, he stared into the Angel dugout, slowing his trot to a walk. He pointed to his wrist and laughed, while the embarrassed Piersall sat motionless in the corner of the dugout, trying unsuccessfully to be inconspicuous. The Yanks went on to lose the game, but Pepi had won the battle of the hot dogs.

Pepitone hit a second unimportant homer in California. The organist that evening was playing different tunes following the announcement of each new batter. After hearing, "Batting fourth for the Yankees, No. 25, Joe Pepitone," I could make out a couple of bars of "That's Amore" being played on the organ, reminding the crowd of Joe's Italian heritage. Joe Garagiola, broadcasting for the Yanks that year, kidded about the mispronunciation of Joe's last name. "I like the way that guy says Pepitone's last name—Joe PepiTONE," mimicking the announcer's mistake of accenting the last syllable instead of the first. Garagiola kidded about it for a few more minutes, along with the organist's rendition of Dean Martin's classic. The next time Pepitone came up, the P.A. man repeated, "Joe PepiTONE," with "That's Amore" again preceding the announcement. Before the organist could finish, Garagiola yelled, "There she goes! That ball is outta here."

All right, Pepi! I thought. A moment later, Garagiola teased, "So Joe PepiTONE hits a home run for the YanKEES." It wasn't an important event, and Garagiola probably doesn't remember it. Pepitone probably never knew of the humor of the evening, but the pleasure of the home run and Garagiola's broadcast that night are still with me.

Pepitone had his share of arguments with umpires, but one incident stands out. It was such an explosive display of anger by Pepi that this chapter would be lacking without some mention of it.

The Yanks were playing a three-game series with the Indians in Cleveland. Pepitone entered the first game slumping with the bat. He came up in the late innings with his team trailing by a run. Luis Tiant was on the mound pitching effectively against the Yanks. With a man on base and two outs, Pepitone hit a drive to right. Rizzuto yelled, "This should tie it up!" The right-fielder went back to the fence and waited. To Phil's amazement and mine, the ball was caught for the final out. A gust of wind had held what looked to be a sure home run. Pepitone was visibly upset, and Tiant, on his way to the dugout, smiled and said something to Joe. He picked the wrong time and person to joke with. Pepitone yelled back in a threatening manner. As play continued, Luis continued joking, standing at the steps of the dugout and yelling out to Joe. Pepi took it in stride.

But Pepi's explosive temper presented itself in full force the next day. Joe was at bat early in the game, and umpire Emmett Ashford was calling balls and strikes. Pepitone took the first pitch for a strike. The next delivery looked outside, but Ashford called it strike two. Joe turned around to argue with Emmett before resuming his batting stance. When the next pitch came home, Joe took it again. He shouldn't have. Ashford called, "Strike three!" Pepi reacted typically. He went face to face with the ump, and it didn't take long for Ashford to give him the heave-ho. Pepi became livid. He went chest to chest with the umpire and kept after him even as Ashford tried to walk away. It took four or five of his teammates to restrain Joe. His shirt ripped open as he struggled to free himself and get at Ashford. When finally Pepi was in control and safely in the dugout, Houk resumed the argument, letting Ashford know what he thought of his eyesight. If it seemed to Joe at the time that the world was against him, at least he knew the Major was on his side.

One of Pepitone's biggest years was 1966. He started off poorly, hitting only five home runs after the first two months. On April 29 in an exhibition game at West Point, he was fined $250 by manager Johnny Keane for leaving the ball park too early. "It was all a misunderstanding," explained Pepi. "I paid the fine and said nothing. Any reports that I made nasty remarks to Johnny are lies." On May 3, he just missed hitting a home run in the ninth, coincidentally with Luis Tiant on the mound. The ball missed the foul pole by inches. Pepi then made an out, leaving the tying run stranded at first.

Another game in May of that year was thrilling. It was one of the last times Roger Maris and Mickey Mantle hit homers in the same game. The Yanks were losing 2–0 when Mick hit his first homer of the season to cut the lead in half. Maris tied it in the seventh with his 250th career homer. In the ninth Pepitone joined the home run barrage with his fourth of the year to win it for the Yanks.

Pepi warmed up in June. On the 7th, he hit a two-run homer, giving him his first RBIs in twelve games and helping Fritz Peterson pick up the victory. Three days later, the Yanks opened a three-game series in Detroit. Pepitone hit a home run in each game. One of his shots was a titanic blast that ricocheted off the facade of the roof in right field. Another came in the eighth inning and proved to be a game winner.

Joe had another surge at the end of the month, hitting two homers in a three-game series against Boston and following with another in a game against the Senators. It gave him a total of fifteen home runs, ten coming in the month of June. Normally, sportswriters would have given Pepi plenty of print in their columns, but his hot bat was superseded by a torrid display by a more popular figure. The revitalized Mick was in the midst of a home run binge that would end with his hitting eight homers in six games. With the popular Mantle again making noise with the lumber, Pepitone's heroics took a back seat.

By All-Star break, Pepi and Mickey were tied for the club lead in homers with eighteen and RBIs with forty-one. Unfortunately for Mickey, he didn't improve much on those figures, a combination of injuries and age slowing him down. In contrast, Pepitone continued producing. He had a big game against Kansas City on July 14, hitting a triple and a mammoth home run to right field as well as scoring three runs. By the end of the month, Joe was among the leaders in home runs with twenty-four. In an interview, Pepitone pointed out, as he often did in his career, that he was finally ready to play up to his capabilities. "I have a lot more confidence now, and I don't think any pitcher can get me out," he said. "I've wasted enough time, and I'm a little tired of hearing people say that I've never come up to my potential. Now I'm bearing down."

Joe slowed down slightly in August, but not much. He hit a home run in a 4–3 defeat in California on the first of the month. About a week later, his two-run homer was the difference in a 2–1 victory for Fritz Peterson. It was Peterson's first victory since Pepi's homer had helped him win during the previous month. Later in August, Pepi proved to skeptics that his new attitude toward the game was no joke. Prior to a game against Kansas City, he asked Houk to start him despite being injured. He collected a pair of hits and three RBIs in a 7–3 win. After the game, a motivated Pepitone revealed why he preferred the field to the bench. "I want to hit at least thirty homers, and I think I have a chance for a hundred RBIs," Joe pointed out. "I can't do it sitting on the bench, so I want to play. It's not as good as I wanted, but at least it is an improvement and will give me new goals to shoot at next year."

On August 26 Pepitone hit his twenty-ninth round-tripper, which surpassed his previous high set in 1964. It was on the same night that Mantle came off the bench after a long absence to hit a game-winning homer off Hank Aguirre, so naturally Joe didn't get much attention in the clubhouse afterward. Two days later, Pepi connected again, giving Peterson a comfortable lead en route to a victory. "I was glad to see Joe hit that homer," Peterson remarked after the game. It's funny how some hitters do well whenever a particular teammate of theirs is on the mound. For Pepitone, Fritz was a good luck charm.

The home run on August 28 was Pepi's last until

his thirty-first and final round-tripper of the season on September 17. He hit it off lefty Jim Kaat with two outs in the ninth inning on the day the Yanks were honoring recently retired Bobby Richardson at the Stadium. Injuries slowed Joe down the final month, but at least he had accomplished one of his goals. Although Pepi didn't reach the one hundred RBI mark, his eighty-three led the club that year.

Nineteen sixty-seven was a disappointing season, especially after his big one the previous year. He batted only .251, but that was no surprise since his average had never been much higher. However, he belted a mere thirteen home runs and drove in sixty-four runs. He scored only forty-five runs, about half of the previous year's total. Although missing thirty games had something to do with his decline in numbers, fans looked forward to a more inspired effort from Pepitone in 1968.

Early bad luck interfered with Joe's chances for rebounding in 1968. In the third game of the season, he fractured his elbow, which kept him out of the lineup for over a month. Upon his return on May 13, Pepi had three hits including two doubles, the first time all year any Yankee had more than one extra-base hit in a game. In the next contest, he picked up his first RBI of the season, along with a single and double. On May 20, on the Bombers' thirty-sixth game, Pepi hit his first homer in the ninth inning, to help Jim Bouton win his first game as a starter in two years. On May 26 he hit a home run in each game of a doubleheader sweep of the Chicago White Sox. Later that week, with lucky Fritz on the mound, Pepi led a come-from-behind victory with a home run off the Tigers' Denny McLain. If Peterson was Pepitone's favorite pitcher to have on the mound, the Tigers must have been his favorite team to hit against.

Whenever Pepi played against them, whether at Yankee Stadium or Detroit, he destroyed them.

Although his injury had deprived him of five weeks' work with the bat, Joe took advantage of his opportunities while he was healthy. He stayed hot in June, hitting a grand slam and a two-run triple to knock in six of the Yanks' runs in a 7–2 victory. Afterward Pepi favored reporters with some amusing comments. When asked why he didn't do as well in every game, Joe quipped that if he did, "I'd be a million-dollar ball player. In fact, if I got two hits a game all season, I'd own this club." On a roll, Pepi kept the floor. "I'm like Samson," he said. "When I let my hair grow long, I feel strong. If this keeps up, my hair will be down my back when the season ends. I'm not going to cut it while I'm hitting good." Of course, these days athletes don't need an excuse to grow their hair long.

It figured that with Pepi hot, injuries would return to plague him. He sustained a muscle pull in his ribs in mid-June and returned to the lineup on the twenty-ninth. After wincing in pain while running to first, he was replaced by a pinch-runner and missed several games again.

Nineteen sixty-eight was a year to forget for Pepi. In a game against the Orioles in early September, he was even replaced by a pinch-hitter for the first time in his career. With the bases loaded and the Yanks protecting a one-run lead, Houk sent up Rocky Colavito against lefty-throwing Pete Richert. The Rock didn't fare any better than Pepi would have, striking out after getting ahead on the count 3–0.

Pepitone played in 106 games in 1968, and some of those were as a pinch-hitter. His 308 bats were 200 fewer than in 1966 and 120 less than in 1967. Yet he still managed to sock 15 home runs and drive in 56 runs. For two-thirds of a season, Pepi produced often. Still, the numbers were disappointing.

In contrast to 1968, Pepi started the 1969 season with a bang. Nine games into the season, he hit a grand slam homer in the tenth inning to beat the Orioles at Yankee Stadium. "I'm glad I could win it for Mel [Stottlemyre] because he's such a nice guy," Pepi said after the game. "I'm also proud to be playing on the same team as Bobby [Murcer]." Those humble words would sound out of place if spoken by a star ball player today. Most of them are too busy talking about their overabundance of talent and undervalued salaries.

At the end of April, Joe did it again with a tenth inning, game-winning homer, beating the Orioles 6–5. He hit it to the opposite field off Pete Richert, the same tough lefty reliever whom Pepi had faced the previous year when he was lifted in favor of slugger Rocky Colavito. Two weeks later Pepi repeated his late-game heroics by hitting home runs to win both games of a doubleheader against California. In the first game, the Yanks were trailing 1–0 against Andy Messersmith, who was baffling the hitters with slow stuff. With two men on base, Pepitone lined an 0–2 pitch into the right-field seats. The Yanks went on to win 3–1. The nightcap was scoreless going into the ninth. When veteran knuckleballer Hoyt Wilhelm was brought in to relieve for the Angels, Pepi hit the first pitch into the right-center-field bleachers. Joe commented about his second homer after the game: "I just had a feeling I might hit one and make it a wonderful day. I almost dropped when I saw it fall into the bleachers. Man, what a feeling."

By mid-May Pepitone already had eleven home runs, four of them late-inning game winners; but he didn't let up. He hit four more before June 8, the day the Yanks retired Mickey Mantle's No. 7 uniform. They were playing a doubleheader that day and Mel Stottlemyre was pitching, so I had three good reasons for being there. I arrived at the Stadium early, but since 60,000 Mantle loyalists had the same idea, the best seat to be found was in the upper deck in right field. During the ceremonies, the announcement of Joe Dimaggio's name sent a ripple of surprise through the crowd. Mickey and Joltin' Joe exchanged plaques along with some words of praise for each other that I couldn't hear over the noisy and excited crowd.

The most memorable part of that day was Pepitone's heroics. Pepi was always popular with the fans, but on that day he seemed to be even more of a crowd favorite. True, he had been hot at the plate, but the atmosphere of the occasion had more to do with it than anything, reminding fans that their long-time hero was gone from the game and it was time they sought someone else to idolize. Having played alongside Mickey for so many years, Pepitone was a natural substitute.

Pepi rose to the occasion. In the first game he launched a three-run homer to right, narrowly missing the upper deck where I was seated. As he rounded the bases, the crowd went wild and didn't stop cheering for a few minutes. The homer was a game-winner, providing the Bombers with all the runs in a 3–1 victory behind Stottlemyre.

Joe hit another round-tripper the next day, a blast into the upper deck for the Yanks' only run in a 7–1 loss to Kansas City. The run gave him seventeen for the year, second best in the league. With more than half the season to go, seventeen was already more than he had hit in each of the previous two years. It seemed certain that the popular Pepi would have his greatest season, but a slump plagued him for the next two weeks. Joe couldn't do anything right, and his frustration came to a head one evening in Boston, which was the turning point of his season and probably his career.

On June 20 the Yankees played the Red Sox in the first game of a three-game series. They loaded the bases in the first inning, bringing cleanup batter Pepitone to the plate. Joe hit the first pitch thrown to him into the right-field bullpen, giving New York a 4–0 lead and Pepi his first homer in almost two weeks.

As luck would have it, it began to rain right after Pepitone's blast. The umpires waited about an hour, and the rain subsided, and so home plate umpire Hank Soar decided to resume play. While the field was being prepared, Phil Rizzuto interviewed Joe. Pepi was optimistic about the game lasting the five innings necessary for it, and his slammer, to be official. He also mentioned that he hoped the homer would get him started with the bat again. "Well, it looks like they're going to get the game in," Rizzuto predicted. "Good luck."

"Thanks a lot, Phil," Pepi answered in good humor.

Well, that conversation must have jinxed it, because a few seconds later the rain began pouring down harder than before. Soar waited an hour and then called the game.

In the clubhouse afterward, Houk complained to reporters about Soar's postponing the game prematurely, and Pepitone was furious. "The ribbies are gone. . . . Suppose I drive in ninety-six runs this year? This will cost me the one hundred RBIs and a lot of money. [Presumably he had an incentive clause in his contract.] We could have kept playing. We often played in worse weather than this."

Houk agreed, a little more diplomatically. "I know the umpires have a tough job, but they were weather forecasting instead of just umpiring. I know we could have been playing at least an hour while we were waiting."

That the Yanks had been forced to play in the rain at Boston the previous year, with Soar as the head umpire, a game in which they had a big lead and eventually lost, made matters worse. "Soar was here last year and made us play the whole game in a downpour!" Pepi cried. "I was in center field, and it was raining so hard I couldn't see the pitcher."

If Pepitone hadn't been struggling at the plate, he might not have taken it so hard. This was one that he would remember for quite awhile, and it didn't take him long to make that evident.

Pepitone played in the last game of the series— one in which he would go 0–15 with the bat. He tapped a foul down the first base line, and coach Ellie Howard picked the ball up, looked at it, and flipped it to home plate ump Art Franz. Without inspecting it, Franz threw the ball back to Red Sox hurler Ray Jarvis. That precipitated a cavalry-like charge from the dugout by Houk, who gave the rookie ump a verbal thrashing in his unique, inimitable style, leading to his inevitable ejection. Howard joined the act, shoving umpire Emmett Ashford in the process.

In a show of such emotional display, how could Pepitone be left out? He seized the occasion to let off some steam that had been building for three days. What better target for his wrath than Hank Soar, who had deprived him of his grand salami? "You screwed up the whole series since you called the game Friday," a sore Pepi told Soar. It wasn't long before Joe joined the Major in the showers. The Yanks won the game, but Soar got off a parting shot afterward. "The Yanks shouldn't kick," he sarcastically told reporters. "I won the game for them!" meaning that Len Boehmer, who replaced Pepitone at first after his ejection, got the game-winning hit in the tenth.

It wasn't funny to Joe. The incident only accentuated the frustration he had been experiencing. Unfortunately, there were even worse times ahead. Pepi struggled for seven more weeks, hitting four home runs and gathering only a handful of RBIs during that time. There was an occasional spark where it looked as though Pepi would be coming out of it. For instance, in a game against Detroit Joe hit a homer off Denny McLain to account for the only run in a 2–1 loss. McLain had won thirty-one the year before and would win another twenty-four in 1969. Pepitone entered the game with only one hit in his last twenty-three at bats. He pulled a shot to right field for a round-tripper in the sixth and doubled to right-center in the eighth. The double is memorable because the ball looked as if it were in the catcher's mitt when he hit it, showing how quick Pepitone's wrists were.

Joe drove in the game winner in early July with a center-field single off Sam McDowell. Later, Pepitone showed that his ever-present sense of humor was as much a part of his personality during rough times as it was during pleasant ones. "I always bear down against Sam," Pepi jested. "I'm afraid of him, that's why."

Joe's woes continued until early August. On the ninth, New York played a doubledip against the A's. Pepi exploded from his slump with five hits, including a home run. It was the best day he had had since his two homers won both games of a doubleheader in mid-May. He also made a spectacular defensive play in the opener when Bert Campaneris, after bunting, slid into first to try to avoid the tag. Pepi had to race in, field the ball, and dive toward the line to nip Campy. "I was scared silly," Joe joked later. "I almost lost my cap, and that would have mussed up my hair."

Joe followed up with another homer against Chuck Dobson the next day. It tied the score, allowing the Yanks to take the lead later and the game 2–1. The home run was his twenty-fourth, and it looked as if Pepitone was poised for a late-season surge that would challenge the career-high thirty-one he hit in 1966.

Then Pepi turned magician. He disappeared, failing to show up at the ball park a few days later. Houk cleared up the mystery only slightly when he spoke to reporters after the game. "Joe has some personal problems," the Major said. "I don't think I should say any more about it. . . . One thing for sure is that we didn't have a fight."

He didn't have Pepitone either, because Joe wasn't at the Stadium the next day when the Yanks lost to the Twins. Houk reiterated what he had said the night before, adding that he expected Pepitone to make the team flight to Chicago that day.

The Yanks played the first game of the series with the White Sox the following night, and Pepi was in the lineup. After New York's 3–2 victory, Pepitone answered reporters' questions politely but was uncharacteristically evasive, shedding no more light on the subject of his mysterious absence. Houk tried to dissuade the press from continuing their interrogation while announcing that Pepi had been docked in pay for missing the two games.

About a week later, Pepitone asked out of the lineup, complaining of a stiff neck and back. He missed the next couple of games as well. Coincidentally, all were against lefty pitchers. At the end of August when the rosters were expanded, the Yankees called up thirteen players from their farm system, and four of them were first basemen. Rumors circulated that perhaps the Yanks had had enough of Joe's frequent dilemmas and were planning to ship him out.

Then it occurred—or to put it more accurately—recurred. On August 29 Pepitone vanished again. This time it was a little different. Joe had showed up at the ball park, only to discover that he had been fined $500. The reason, as Houk told reporters later, was because Pepitone had left the Stadium in the middle of the game the previous day, in spite of the manager's instructions to stay on the bench for the entire game. When Pepi was informed of the fine, he took a walk. No manager was ever more patient or more loyal to his players than Houk, but when he faced the press, it was obvious that the Major had had enough. "Joe's only the second player I ever fined," he said. "I hate to levy fines since I don't think it does any good, but no player is going to shaft me!"

The next day the situation remained the same, although it was made known that Pepitone had been in contact with the Yankees' executive Mike Burke, saying at the meeting that he was "not psychologically ready to rejoin the team." A couple of business associates attended the meeting with Joe, who apparently was ready to start a clothes and beauty business. That may have been the reason for Joe's rebellious attitude since any kind of publicity could be lucrative for his store. Perhaps Joe's new entrepreneurial interests necessitated his absence from the team for awhile. Or maybe it was the prospect of

Pepi signs an autograph on September 2, 1969, the day of his return to the club following his second walkout. Joe finished the season, and his career with the Yanks was finished as well. [AP/Wide World Photos]

being on his own in a non-baseball enterprise which which Joe hoped would be a big money maker that prompted his independent attitude.

Whether his prospective venture into the business world had been the immediate reason for his unprofessional conduct is uncertain. In a press conference on September 2, Pepitone denied that money matters were the cause and put the blame on marital problems instead. However, he hinted that baseball wasn't as much fun as it used to be. After admitting he was wrong, Pepi added, "I'd rather be a peddler in the street making $100 a week and be happy than make $40,000 a year and not be happy."

It was over. Houk's fine stood, and Pepitone was reinstated before the game against Seattle that night. But if the incident was over, so too was Pepitone's career with the Yankees. If the team executives had not already made up their minds about trading Joe, his second walkout certainly convinced them, although they wouldn't get rid of him before the season ended.

Joe finished the last month uneventfully, although I remember his last round-tripper was a 1–0 game winner. That homer gave him twenty-seven for the season, enough to lead the team and to be among the league leaders. Without the distractions of the last two months, Joe could have had an outstanding year. If nothing else, Pepi showed in 1969 that when he was able to concentrate on baseball, he was one of the best in the game. The grand slammer snatched away from him by the rain in Boston in mid-June might have been pivotal in Joe's downfall. Had it stood, it might have snapped Pepi out of his slight slump and kept his motivation high.

If the Yankees were unfair to Bobby Murcer when they traded him in 1975, as I felt, Pepitone certainly deserved his fate. The Yanks had a young, impressionable team, and the fear was that Joe would become a distracting, negative influence on them. Mike Burke and company had no choice but to say goodbye to Pepi. If there was anyone to blame, Pepitone had only himself to point to.

Joe retired from baseball during the 1973 season after playing in only thirty-four games for the Cubs. He had thought about retiring the previous year and in fact announced to the press he was quitting in early May 1972. "It's no longer fun playing baseball," he told reporters. "This has been on my mind for six years. I just lost interest in baseball." He changed his mind, as the unpredictable Pepitone did often in his career, and finished the 1972 season.

After he retired, Pepi played professional ball in Japan, but that didn't last long. The discipline on the Japanese ball club was probably too much for Joe to handle. Some time later he started a softball team and fooled around with that for awhile.

That's the last I heard of Joe Pepitone until I saw him on television in 1989. He wasn't singing this time but was being interviewed from prison where he was doing time for a drug possession conviction. It was one of many mistakes in his lifetime, but this was the biggest. He had enjoyed some privileges as a Yankee and an ex-Yankee, but breaking the law and going unpunished was not one of them. Joe had to pay the price.

Pepi cried during that interview, and I was sad for him. He was a victim of his own personality, and it was possible to feel sorry for him without excusing what he had done. I wish him my best and hope that now that he is out of prison the rest of his life will be more tranquil and stable.

Pepitone appears at Brooklyn Criminal Court in 1988 to hear his sentence for a misdemeanor drug conviction. [AP/Wide World Photos]

I saw Joe again during Old-Timers' Day at Yankee Stadium in 1991. As the television camera zoomed in the dugout for the first time, who else but Joe Pepitone would be standing directly in front of the camera, talking to another Old Timer. That he was positioned in the part of the dugout where the TV crew could focus on him best was, of course, a coincidence. Later, when Frank Messer announced his name to the crowd, Pepi ran onto the field with clenched fists high in the air, as if to signify, "Yes, I'm back!"

I won't let the mistakes he made allow me to forget my wonderful memories of Pepitone playing baseball, and I hope other fans won't either. When we were kids, my dad used to tell us that if a person does something bad, that doesn't make him a bad person. Whenever I think about Joe, I'll keep that in mind.

Thanks for the memories, Pepi!

CHAPTER FOUR

MEL STOTTLEMYRE

Sinking the Opposition

WHITEY FORD? EDDIE LOPAT? RED RUFF-
ing? Allie Reynolds? Ron Guidry? Who was the greatest Yankee pitcher of all time? Most Yankee fans
choose from among those aforementioned names in
answering that question. Not me. In my opinion, Mel
Stottlemyre belongs at the top of the list.

A comparison of statistics is unavoidable to sat-
isfy critics who will disagree with my choice of
Stottlemyre. On the following page is a chart listing
the pitchers, along with their Yankee career stats, for
what many baseball experts would agree are the most
important categories.

To look at statistics without carefully analyzing
them would be meaningless. So a careful comparison must be made.

Decisions

Stottlemyre's winning percentage is unimpres-
sive, especially alongside the other Yankee greats.
The reason, of course, has to do with the teams they

Mel Stottlemyre [National Baseball Library, Cooperstown, New York]

	Stottlemyre	Ford	Reynolds	Ruffing	Lopat	Guidry
won	164	236	131	234	123	170
lost	139	106	60	129	75	91
percent	.541	.690	.686	.645	.621	.651
starts	356	438	209	400	202	323
complete games	152	156	96	262	91	95
shutouts	40	45	21	40	20	26
hits per game	8.2	7.9	7.9	8.5	9.1	8.3
walks per game	2.7	3.1	4.3	3.0	2.4	2.4
K's per game	4.2	5.6	5.1	4.3	3.0	6.7
ERA	2.97	2.74	3.31	3.43	3.18	3.29
opponents' average	.245	.235	.238	.248	.262	.244
20-win seasons	3	2	1	4	1	3

played for. In Stottlemyre's eleven-year stay with the Yanks, only in 1964—his rookie year—was he on a pennant winner, and he only played half a season. In contrast, all the other Yankee greats accumulated winning season after winning season on Yankee teams that missed playing in the Fall Classic only once or twice during their New York careers. Naturally, it's easier to win when your team is a winner, but Mel had a .541 lifetime winning percentage at a time when the Yanks had a percentage of below .500. This is a telling sign of his greatness.

Further evidence can be found by looking at the careers of Reynolds, Ruffing, and Lopat when they pitched on weaker ball clubs. Reynolds had a winning percentage of .520 with Cleveland compared to .686 with the Yanks. Ruffing's percentage was a dismal .296 with Boston, and he had a losing record in each of the five full seasons he played for the Red Sox. Yet, incredibly, he had fourteen winning seasons with the Yanks, accumulating a whopping .645 percentage. Lopat's percentage with Chicago was .501 in 99 games, but he soared to .621 in 198 games with the Bronx Bombers. Although their pitching talents had a lot to do with the Yanks winning so many pennants, it's hard to believe those same pitchers were that much less effective on other ball clubs. It is more likely that the general ineptitude of those teams resulted in poorer seasons for Reynolds, Ruffing, and Lopat.

It wasn't only that Stottlemyre lacked enough powerful hitters who could generate runs the way Ruth, Gehrig, Dimaggio, Henrich, Berra, and a youthful Mantle had done in the past, that caused him to win fewer games. True as that may be, the Yanks also lacked quality defensive ball players during his tenure, which also probably had much to do with his record. When Clete Boyer left the game in the mid-sixties, Mel had the likes of Bobby Cox, Bobby Murcer, Tommy Tresh, Jerry Kenney, and Celerino Sanchez tending third base. As they fielded their positions, "the hot corner" got even hotter. At shortstop, Bobby Murcer, Tommy Tresh, Jerry Kenney, and Gene Michael took turns, and none of them will make the Hall of Fame for their efforts with the glove. Neither will Horace Clarke, who took over the second base position for many years after Bobby Richardson retired. Clarke was a decent hitter, but his fielding left much to be desired. Yankee fans were relieved when sure-handed Willie Randolph took

over in the mid-seventies. At first base, Joe Pepitone
was good with the glove, but for a couple of seasons
he was forced to play the outfield in deference to
Mantle and his tired legs. I love the Mick, but he
looked out of place at first.

For a sinkerball pitcher like Stottlemyre, it's to
his credit that he did so well with the defense that
surrounded him in the infield. When Mel got into a
jam, he couldn't rely on striking out the opposition
as often as a Ford, Reynolds, or Guidry might. Instead, he relied on his descending fastballs, hoping
to entice overly aggressive hitters to beat the ball
on the ground, setting up double plays. The problem, however, was that his fielders couldn't always
be counted on to make the double play. They had
enough trouble getting one out at a time, so Mel lost
ball games in situations where better infielders would
have made him a winner. Had Boyer, Rizzuto, Martin, or Richardson been Stot's teammates during
his entire career, he would have won many more
games.

Games Started and Completed

Only Ford and Ruffing from our select group
started more games for the Yankees than Stottlemyre
did. Of the games that he started, Mel's percentage of
games completed is an outstanding .421. Only Ruffing's .655 was far better, but Red pitched from the
twenties through the forties, a time when it was rare
to pull a starting pitcher from the game when he was
winning. During Mel's career, relief specialists were a
big part of a manager's game plan. (I'm reminded
of an amusing but appropriate comment made by
Joe Dimaggio at an Old Timer's Day celebration of
the fiftieth anniversary of his fifty-six-game hitting
streak. He mentioned how Marius Russo pitched a

nine-inning victory in one of those games. "I only mention that he pitched nine innings," Joe kidded, "because today they consider that such a great feat!") Although Lindy McDaniel and Sparky Lyle were often used by Houk, Stot usually finished what he started. Once after a game the Yanks won behind Mel, the Major was asked why he hadn't brought in a reliever late in the game. "He's my best pitcher," Houk stated. "If he can't get them out, who will?"

Shutouts

Don't look only at the forty shutouts Stottlemyre threw, which puts him in a tie for second behind Whitey Ford on the all-time Yankee list. That's impressive for sure, but consider too that his rate of shutouts thrown—one in every 8.9 games—is better than that of any other Yankee great. Ford's rate was one in every 9.8 games; Ruffing's and Reynold's one in every 10.1 games; and Guidry, one in every 12.4 games.

Hits per game and opponents' average

Stottlemyre wasn't the leader in these categories, but he wasn't last either. Only Ford and Reynolds did appreciably better, possibly because they were strike-out pitchers and didn't have to rely on their defense as much as sinkerballer Mel. Many balls that Stot-tlemyre's mates should have reached made their way to the outfield.

Base-on-balls and strikeouts per game

Many experts would argue that the number of strikeouts accumulated throughout a pitcher's career should not be considered in determining his effectiveness. They would say that if a hitter makes an out on a fly ball or ground ball, he's as out as if he had fanned. Even if you don't agree, a truly better way than looking at strikeouts in an isolated context is to compare his rate of strikeouts with his rate of issuing walks. The better pitchers have a higher strikeout to walk rate. Stottlemyre's strikeout rate was 4.2 per game, quite respectable for a pitcher who normally relied on ground balls to win games. Next to his walk rate of 2.7 per game, though, it looks even better. It gives him a +1.5 strikeout/walk difference per game, better than the other Yankees except for Ford and Guidry.

ERA

The average number of runs allowed in a game that can be attributed to the pitcher's mistakes and not to his teammates should be considered more than any other stat, for allowing as few runs, not hits, per game as possible is the overall objective of any hurler. If a pitcher gives up twenty hits and allows no runs, he did as effective a job for his team as one who pitched a no-hitter. The ERA should not be the sole factor, only the most important.

In my book, any starter who pitches a considerable length of time and has an ERA of under 3.00 should be eligible for the Hall of Fame. (When Tom Seaver made Cooperstown in a landslide vote, a New York paper mentioned that his lifetime 2.86 ERA was the third lowest of all hurlers since 1920 who pitched over 2,000 innings. Stottlemyre's 2.97 ERA, only slightly higher than Tom Terrific's, was obtained after pitching over 2,600 innings.) But since Mel did it on teams with infielders playing musical chairs with their positions, he should be a shoe-in. Ford's 2.74 was indeed remarkable, but his defense robbed opposing hitters more often than Stottlemyre's did. That does not detract from Ford's accomplishment, but

Whitey is in the Hall of Fame. Mel is the only other starter who pitched regularly for the Yanks for ten or more seasons and finished with an ERA of under 3.00, and that is a reason why he belongs in Cooperstown as well.

Twenty-win seasons

Stottlemyre had three of them, and no other Yankee had more than Ruffing's four. Guidry matched Mel's total, but imagine how many years Stottlemyre would have won twenty games if he had pitched during the Ruffing or Guidry eras. Considering his teams' poor capacity for scoring runs and making the plays on the field, it's amazing Mel had any twenty-win seasons.

There are several reasons fans don't usually think of Mel Stottlemyre as being the greatest of Yankee hurlers. First, Stottlemyre threw sinkers, not smoke, and fireball pitchers generally are remembered longer and respected more than those who didn't throw as hard. Mel also had a low-key personality. He was genuinely modest, never beating his own drum, and this made it harder for him to gain national recognition at a time when Yankee teams were drawing little attention. Even his name is not conducive to his being called the best when compared to such colorful ones as Whitey, Red, the Chief, or Louisiana Lightning.

But the main reason Stottlemyre isn't remembered as the best is that he played for a team that was at its worst. Known for their winning tradition and proud past, the Yankees suffered through their toughest times from the mid-sixties to mid-seventies, and Stottlemyre was part of it. He pitched like an All-Star but is remembered as just another player on those mediocre Yankee teams.

That Mel was the greatest is certainly debatable, and some probably would object to my excluding the likes of Vic Raschi, Lefty Gomez, or Bob Sharkey from a comparative analysis. All were great pitchers, and, in a way, insisting that one stands out above all the rest seems a little childish. I would argue, however, that Stot should share the glory equally with the others. To choose Mel as the premier Yankee hurler is no less reasonable than to choose anyone else.

Ralph Houk, who managed both Ford and Stottlemyre, once stated, "Mel and Whitey are the two best pitchers I have ever seen for getting the out they had to get." Another time he commented, "He's as good as any right-handed pitcher I've ever seen here [Yankee Stadium]. Yes, I'm including the Reynoldses, Raschis, and the rest. Mel is quite a pitcher in any league and at any time. Don't forget he's pitching for a club without the power and defense of those old Yankee teams." No higher praise from any better source could ever be found to attest to Stottlemyre's greatness.

Critics of Stottlemyre often point to his disastrous 1966 season. How could anyone who lost twenty games in a season be included among the best? The problem with that argument is that the statistics don't show that Mel pitched well enough to win about a dozen of the games he lost. You'd think a pitcher who lost twenty games would have an abysmal ERA, but Mel's was a respectable 3.80 at the end of 1966. Keep in mind, too, that a manager would be inclined to pull a pitcher from his starting rotation if he were constantly ineffective. Stot didn't miss a turn.

Perhaps that helps to show that only a *good* pitcher is capable of losing twenty games in a season.

The manager usually sticks with a good hurler, either because he's pitching well but is experiencing tough luck, or because he believes the pitcher will return to his proper form. With Houk it was a combination of both. Stottlemyre was still his best pitcher, winning twelve games that year, the most on his staff. Additionally, Mel was beset with bad luck, especially during the first half of the season. It must have prompted Houk to glance into the opponents' dugout now and then, looking for any players who might be sticking pins into Stottlemyre look-alike dolls. Such voodoo techniques wouldn't have been any more effective against Mel than the hard luck he faced that year.

Stottlemyre's first full season had been a dazzling success the previous year. He won twenty games and led the league in complete games and innings pitched. He began the 1966 season in similar fashion, accumulating a 5–3 record after the first two months along with a 1.91 ERA. As if to signal worse times to come, Mel's early success that season was limited, due to his losing some well-pitched ball games. His first loss was a 3–1 decision, followed by a 2–1 defeat. He lost his only game in May by a score of 4–2. In two games in which he pitched and was not involved in the decision, the Yankees lost 3–2 and 2–1. With any luck he could have been 8–1 or 7–2 by the end of May.

He continued pitching well in June, but his record suffered nonetheless. On June 5 he pitched six innings, giving up two earned runs, but he was not credited with a decision. In his next appearance he lost a 2–1 heartbreaker, and after winning 5–2 he was again a victim of a 2–1 setback, giving up only four hits in a frustrating, route-going performance.

Things continued to sour for Stottlemyre, and by mid-June his record had plummeted to 7–11. On July

20 Mel blanked Kansas City 4–0. Not one to ever give excuses before, Mel spoke to reporters candidly after the game. "I'm not alibiing, but things have been happening to me this year that never happened to me before," he said. "Balls bouncing through the infield or blooping in, usually at a time when it hurts. I have to get double plays to be really effective, and this time I got them."

When Stot beat California 9–1 in his next start, it looked as though he might have turned things around. He lost his next start, however, when the White Sox shut out the Yankees. The rest of the season was a struggle for him, and he won only three more games. One of them was memorable.

The Yanks were playing the Angels in Anaheim in early August. Mel was matched against Dean Chance, that old Yankee-killer. The Dean wasn't much of a killer that day, lasting only three innings and giving up seven runs against a team living up to their nickname, the Bombers, for once that year. The rare display of power was led by none other than Stottlemyre himself, whose two-run homer was the only round-tripper of the game. His pitching prowess overshadowed his hitting: He threw a nifty two-hit shutout, with harmless singles by Jose Cardenal and Bobby Knoop, the only Angels who reached base. After the 9–0 blowout, Mel said, "I was throwing better than I have all year. I began to get my curve ball over and was using a changeup successfully. I would say it was my best game."

As big a nemesis as Chance had been against the Yankees—he entered the season with a seven-game winning streak against them—Stottlemyre was just as tough on California during his career. His two-hit masterpiece was his second shutout of the season against them, and it ran his winning streak against the Angels to six. He continued his mastery of the Halo-men throughout the remainder of his career. In July of 1972 Mel frustrated Angel batters with a four-hit shutout at Yankee Stadium. It was his fourth blanking of California that year and his fifth straight against them, running a string of forty-six scoreless innings in the process. No other pitcher before or since has had as much success against the Angels. Mel was asked once for his explanation. "I can't explain the way I pitch against this club. I keep beating them. I guess there's something psychological about it now. I know I face them with a lot of confidence, while they are probably a little short of confidence against me."

When Mel lost to California 3–1 toward the end of the 1973 season, it was the first loss against them in six years and left him with an incredible lifetime record of 19–4. "It had to happen sometime," Mel philosophized. "I guess the law of averages was operating against me, too." How happy Angel fans must have been when Stottlemyre retired the following year.

The home run that Stot hit on that August day in 1966 was his third homer in only his second full season. Mel was a tough out at the plate throughout his career, and he proved it in several situations.

One was against the White Sox in 1969. The Yanks were tied 2–2 when Stot singled in the seventh and came around to score the go-ahead run. Chicago tied the score, and the Yanks were up in the eighth. With Wilbur Wood on the mound, they got their leadoff man on, but the next two batters couldn't advance him. Houk let Stot hit for himself, and he crushed the first knuckleball thrown to him into the left-field seats, winning the game 5–3. It was his fourth career home run, and after the game he reviewed his previous three to reporters. "I hit a homer against Chicago in the Stadium, then had the inside-the-park grand slam against Bill Monboquette and the Red Sox. The last one was hit in California, but I don't remember too much about it. This one I'll remember."

In a game against Minnesota in 1972, Mel was locked in a pitching duel with Bert Blyleven. In the seventh with a man on, Blyleven leveled Stot with a fastball zooming in toward his shoulders. "I don't know how I got out of the way," Mel said later. "That's the closest I have ever come to getting hit. I'm glad he did it, however, for he woke me up at the plate."

À la Reggie Jackson, Stottlemyre stepped back into the batter's box and ripped a double to left-center, scoring the winning run in a 5–3 victory.

No one appreciated Mel's overall athleticism more than Houk. "It goes to show how a pitcher can help himself," preached the Major once after Stot helped win a game with his bat. "Mel is a real good athlete. He can pitch, of course, but he can help himself with the bat, fielding and even running the bases. He's just an all-around ball player."

One of Stottlemyre's last losses in 1966 best typifies the kind of year he and the Yankees had. It came in early September against the pennant-bound Orioles. They lost the game 3–2 when Clete Boyer misplayed a double play ball that allowed the winning run to score. The route-going loss by Mel plunged the Yankees into last place. It was the first time since 1913 that any Yankee team had ever been in last place that late in the year. When they finished in the cellar at the end of the season, it was the first time since 1912.

Stot fared much better in 1967 while the Yanks' record remained almost identical. Although they finished ninth that year, the Bombers lost ninety games, one more than the previous year. On a team that finished eighteen games below .500, Stottlemyre managed a 15–15 record with an ERA of 2.96 (despite being hampered by shoulder problems). His statistics weren't good enough to warrant Cy Young consideration; but, bearing in mind that he pitched for a Yankee team playing possibly the worst baseball in its history, Mel probably deserved it.

Mel's best season came the following year when he won twenty-one games and allowed only 2.45 earned runs per game. It would have earned him the Cy Young almost any other year he pitched; but, as luck would have it, McLain won thirty-one.

Stot got off to a fast start in 1968, and when he won a 1–0 game on May 11 against Boston's Jose Santiago, breaking Santiago's twelve-game winning streak, it was already his third shutout and fourth complete game. He fanned ten Red Sox batters while walking only two. Boston had beaten him four times consecutively the previous year, making the victory for Stottlemyre even sweeter. Unfortunately, he was bombed when he faced them again in Boston the following week.

Stot's next win came on May 21 in Washington. He gave up only one run in a game in which he singled and scored one of the Yankees' two runs. Mel was winning games with the usual lack of support from the Yankee hitters. When he lost 1–0 to Mickey Lolich and the Tigers at the end of the month, it was the third time he had been involved in a 1–0 contest, having won the previous two.

In the Tigers game, the Yanks had a golden opportunity to tie and go ahead in the eighth inning. Ellie Rodriguez opened the frame with a single and moved to third when pinch-hitter Charlie Smith did the same, but Horace Clarke struck out and Roy White popped out. Mantle was intentionally walked, of course, and Lolich retired Andy Kosco to end the game. It was typical of the kind of wasted opportunities the Yanks of the late sixties were noted for, and it must have frustrated Stottlemyre to no end, although reporters could never get him to put the blame on his teammates.

When Mel defeated Baltimore on a four-hitter in another close contest in mid-July, it marked the mid-season point. The Yanks were 36–43, but Mel had the best first half of his career. It was his eleventh victory, and the eleventh time in eighteen starts that he had gone the distance. The win stopped a personal eight-game losing streak against the Orioles, whom he found difficult to beat throughout his career. The All-Star nominee expressed his happiness to reporters afterward. "I was really up for this game. I was getting tired of losing to Baltimore and, more important, I wanted to go into the All-Star break with a good effort behind me. It makes you feel more like you really belong when you win your last one."

Mel, the ace of the staff, was often matched against the best pitcher on opposing ball clubs, making winning even more difficult. More often than not, Stottlemyre prevailed. In a game on July 26 he was locked in a pitching duel with Sam McDowell but wound up the winner, shutting out the Indians despite ten strikeouts by Sudden Sam. In talking about his performance, Stottlemyre later said, "This was the first time I used a changeup against the Indians. The Indians hadn't seen me throw it, so when I found I could use it effectively, I used it quite a bit and got a lot of outs on it. That made them look for a fourth pitch and, at the same time, made my other pitches more effective." Stot's knowledge of the game and his ability to modify his style and pitch selection when necessary explains why he endured as one of the top pitchers in the league as long as he did, whereas the departure from the top ranks by others like McDowell, who were more throwers than pitchers, was more "sudden."

Another great matchup late that year was Mel versus the Tigers' Denny McLain. Denny was the league's winningest pitcher with twenty-eight so far, and he was unbeaten on the road. The Yanks were out of the pennant race, but there were close to thirty thousand fans at the ball park to see the game, which proved as exciting as anticipated. McLain pitched a marvelous game, giving up only five hits and two runs. It wasn't good enough, though, as Stottlemyre allowed only four hits and one run, a solo homer by Willie Horton (Horton had beaten Mel 1–0 earlier in the year with a home run). That Mantle went hitless was not so upsetting to me that day. In the dugout, Stot admitted to the significance of the game. "I would have to say this was my most satisfying victory of the year. When I knew I was going to face McLain, I was glad, especially since it is always a challenge when you face one of the best." Manager Houk sang the praises of his pitcher to reporters. "That Stottlemyre is really something. Any time he goes to that mound, you know somebody is going to get a battle. I didn't call the bullpen once all day."

Stottlemyre matched his winning output of the previous season when he defeated the Oakland A's in early August with a brilliant six-hit zip. The shutout was his fifth, which was a career high at the time (he went on to pitch one more that year). The game was marked by a rain delay of more than an hour and a half in the fourth inning, which for a control pitcher like Stot is usually a problem. Even he had difficulty explaining his success. "I was surprised I was able to come back without any trouble. I was afraid I might be a little stiff, but I wasn't."

Mel picked up a win a couple of weeks later with another blanking, whitewashing Minnesota 5–0. It was sweet revenge for Stot, who had been knocked out in the second inning in his previous start against the Twins. He dominated Twins' batters with a sinkerball that resulted in sixteen ground ball outs. Incredibly, it was the seventh time he had given up fewer than five hits in a game that year.

On September 13 Mel picked up his twentieth victory for the second time in his career, defeating Washington 4–2 in a complete-game performance. "I wanted my twentieth to be a complete game," Mel said afterward. "It seems like a long time since spring training, but I still think about how worried I was. I had never had any arm or health problems until last year, then I had tendinitis in my shoulder." When Mel won his twenty-first on September 24, beating the Indians 5–1, it set a personal career high for wins, along with complete games with nineteen, more than most Yankee pitchers, including Ford, had ever finished in one year. Stot pitched with impeccable control, allowing only 2.1 walks and a mere 7.8 hits per game. Along with his six shutouts and low ERA they were the best overall stats Stot would ever produce in a season.

In 1969 Stottlemyre accomplished what only a few Yankee hurlers have ever done: He won twenty games for the second consecutive season. No other pinstripe pitcher has done it since, and with the Yanks playing under .500 ball in 1969, it makes his achievement that much more remarkable.

As he did in 1968, Mel started 1969 on fire, winning his first five starts, including a one-hit shutout in Detroit. Every great pitcher flirts with a no-hitter at least once during his career, and that game in early April against the World Champion Tigers and Cy Young award winner McLain was the closest Mel ever came to perfection. He allowed only a fifth inning, two-out double by Jim Northrup. Errors by Clarke and Murcer allowed two other Tigers to reach base, and that was it. Stot even contributed with the bat, singling and scoring one of the Yanks' four runs.

Stottlemyre won his fifth straight on April 25, going the distance in a 7–2 thrashing of the Orioles in Baltimore. With McLain having won thirty the previous year, some were already beginning to wonder if Mel could do the same. "Look, I just take them one at a time," he responded to reporters. "You have to be lucky to talk about twenty-five or thirty, so let's just hope the luck holds out."

Fate had different ideas. Mel proceeded to lose his next three decisions. He bounced back, though, with a defeat of the White Sox on a relatively new grass for American Leaguers—the artificial surface. He was asked afterward whether he felt the field helped or hindered his performance. "I am basically a low-ball pitcher, so if some balls might skip through the infield faster off me, there will be others that get to the fielders quicker and become double plays." What he didn't mention was that his infielders had limited range to start with, which meant that more balls would be shooting through the infield than with other teams, while the double-play combo, with Clarke at the pivot, would usually fail in their attempts even with the extra time.

When Stottlemyre shut out Detroit again toward the end of June, it was his tenth victory and twelfth complete game in a score of starts. Afterward, he disclosed why it had been difficult for him to achieve number ten, having failed in his previous three attempts. His words revealed the pressure he and other Yankee hurlers must have felt trying to win games on a team providing little support. "I had been trying to pitch too fine to avoid mistakes in close games," Mel said. "The five-run lead was a big help. When you are working with a lead, you can relax and let them hit the ball. Most of our games are one-runners. I go out trying to hold the opposition to one run at the most. You always have in the back of your mind that one bad pitch can beat you, but with a lead it is entirely different."

Stot stayed hot in July, winning all his starts prior to the All-Star break. He defeated the Orioles 3–2 on July 2 for his eleventh victory, toughing out a first and second, nobody out jam in the ninth by getting the dangerous Boog Powell on a pop-up and clutch hitter Brooks Robinson on a double-play grounder. On July 6 Mel won his twelfth, defeating the Indians in a game in which opposing pitcher Sam McDowell had a few arguments with plate umpire Don Denkinger. "Sam did a lot of beefing, which might have helped me," Mel explained. "I never beef. The umpires don't beat you." It was a comment typical of Stottlemyre. His character never allowed him to use an alibi when he was losing nor brag when winning.

Stot rolled along to number thirteen in his next outing, defeating the Senators 4–3, stranding the tying and winning base runners in the final inning. Although it had been a struggle for Mel throughout, Houk again stuck with his veteran sinkerball thrower during the nail-biting ninth, reiterating afterward what he had said earlier. "He's the best pitcher I've got. If he feels good, has good stuff and can't get them out, who will?"

The complete game was his fifteenth, the most in the league, and the win was the first by any Yankee in seven games. He picked up another victory against the Senators in his following start, shutting them out on three hits while walking only two. It was his first start prior to the All-Star game. Since he was leading the league in complete games, victories, and shutouts, Stottlemyre was the logical selection as starting pitcher for the American League.

Considering Mel had the best first half of his career with a 14–7 record, the second half had to be a bit of a disappointment. He gained only six more victories. He picked up a couple of wins soon after the All-Star break, including a 2–1 squeaker against Reggie Jackson and the Athletics on Old Timers' Day at Yankee Stadium. He allowed only four hits and at one point retired twenty in a row, handing out 0–4s to the likes of Jackson, Sal Bando, and Rick Monday. That would be his last good outing for quite awhile. In a game on August 23 against the Minnesota Twins, Mel was attacked in more ways than one, getting hit with a shot off the bat of Ted Uhlaender on the very first pitch of the game that put him on the ground. It should have served as an omen to Stot, for when he resumed pitching, he was blasted, giving up five runs and not lasting past that first inning en route to an 8–3 loss. It was his third consecutive failure to pick up his seventeenth victory.

After finally winning his seventeenth in his next start with a 6–3 victory over Chicago, Mel admitted he had been worrying. "I hate to admit it, but I guess I've been pressing," he said. "It was beginning to bug me. I know I haven't been right. I've been too erratic, and my fastball hasn't been sinking." Mel also admitted that the leg was bothering him when he tried to continue pitching against the Twins his previous outing. "Actually, the leg was numb so I thought it didn't hurt," he commented. "Then the numbness began to wear off, and it really hurt."

With the victory, Mel once again took aim at twenty wins. He lost a 2–1 heartbreaker to Cleveland's McDowell on September 5, although he did pick up his twenty-second complete game, still a league high. He won his next start but was not involved in the decision in the following one. In that game, Stot went into the eighth inning with a four-hit shutout against the Red Sox but lost his control and composure. He walked the bases loaded, forcing Houk to go to his bullpen. Reliever Jack Aker allowed two of the runners to score, tying the game. The Yanks scored a run in the bottom of the ninth, defeating Boston 3–2. With two weeks left in the season and four more starts, at most, remaining, it looked like Stottlemyre might have trouble reaching the twenty-win plateau for the second straight season, an accomplishment that had looked like a certainty just before the All-Star break. It would be especially difficult since Mel's anxiety seemed to be affecting his performance.

When he fell behind the Senators on September 18 at the Stadium, it looked gloomy for Stottlemyre fans. Trailing 3–2 in the eighth, the Yanks loaded the bases with two outs. John Ellis singled to left, scoring two runs, and provided Stot with a rare come-from-behind victory. It took a lot of pressure off Mel, knowing he had three more chances to get one more. "I'll pitch him with four days rest twice and three days rest the last day," Houk stated. "That should give him a fair shot."

Stottlemyre would wait until his last start to win his twentieth game, and it wasn't easy. Actually, once again the Yanks had to come from behind, this time in the last inning. Trailing 2–1, Jerry Kenney singled with two men on, tying the score, and Brooks Robinson, of all people, threw away a Thurman Munson grounder, bringing in the winning run. It was poetic justice that the Yanks, who had let Stottlemyre down so many times in the past, would come through for him in his last two victories. A relieved Stottlemyre talked about the win later. "I would have been very disappointed if I hadn't won twenty, but only because I had been so close to it for so long. That ninth inning was the longest of my life."

Houk was equally elated for his star pitcher. "It's hard to explain how a guy like Mel is to manage," he said. "I'm tickled to see him get twenty. He certainly deserved it and with a little luck would have had it a long time ago. Some of the ones he lost were real tough."

Despite his poor second half of the season, it was quite a year for Stottlemyre. Along with his twenty wins, he led the league with twenty-four complete games, three of them shutouts. He pitched 303 innings, a career high, and was the first Yankee to do that in more than forty years. Although his ERA jumped during his slump, it was still one of the best in the league at 2.82. Nineteen sixty-nine was another great year for Stottlemyre, and his last great one.

The remaining years produced somewhat mediocre records, although they were not without significance in other respects. For instance, in 1971 he pitched a career-high seven shutouts; he duplicated that notable feat in 1972. He got his first that year in early May, defeating the Angels 5–0 at the Stadium. Stot pitched two consecutive shutouts later that month, whitewashing the Red Sox for his third blanking. Then came a road trip in July when Mel pitched better than he ever had. He lost a 1–0 thriller to Oakland, giving up the only run in the three games he pitched during the trip. He defeated Minnesota 1–0 in an eleven-inning nail-biter against Bert Blyleven. The game was won on a home run by Bernie Allen, but Mel was yanked by Houk in favor of Sparky Lyle and lost credit for the shutout.

Stottlemyre followed with a 5–0 blanking of California, giving up seven hits and no walks. It gave him a string of twenty-two consecutive scoreless innings on the road trip and his fourth shutout of the season. He talked after the game about how he tried to keep his concentration with a rare five-run lead. "I made believe I had a one-run lead," he said, "because that keeps you bearing down all the time. I don't like to start coasting."

When the Yanks returned home, Mel stayed hot, picking on the Angels again for his fifth shutout. He was helped out by four double plays. He pitched poorly after that, winning only once in more than a month. Houk later admitted that using his ace too frequently in a year when his team was still in the pennant race late in the season may have been the reason. "I may be the cause of Mel's problem," he said once. "I may have overworked him in that tough stretch of doubleheaders. I'm convinced that I wore him down."

When Stot finally won with a 4–0 blanking of the White Sox on September 1, 1972, he offered a different explanation of his previous problems. "I finally found the source of my trouble," he said. "I have been overstriding, and that has affected my pitches, especially the breaking stuff. I tried cutting down my stride, and it worked."

He may have been right, for he pitched well the remainder of the season. Stot zipped by Detroit for his seventh shutout, not allowing a walk and giving up only three hits.

The most important game Mel pitched in 1972 came against the Orioles at Yankee Stadium in mid-September. The Yanks were still in the hunt and were counting on their ace to shoot down the league-leading Birds. Stottlemyre gave up a three-run homer to Boog Powell in the first inning for the only runs Baltimore needed in a 3–1 victory behind Jim Palmer. After the game, Mel was visibly upset and wouldn't say much to reporters, except to snap uncharacteristically, "I don't want —— long interviews. You guys will write what you want anyway, so one question and out."

Whatever caused Stottlemyre to become so terse and impolite, it certainly wasn't selfishness. He had let the team down at a time when they needed a win badly, although giving up three runs can hardly classify as letting the team down. Also, because it was rare that September games meant anything to the Yankees during his pitching career, the loss made him feel even worse. With the loss, the New Yorkers fell two and one-half games behind the Orioles and would never get any closer.

It was a disappointing year for Mel. For once the roles were reversed, with Stot pitching mediocre ball (14–18 record; 3.22 ERA), while the Yanks were contenders until late in the season. As he remarked once in September, "This has been a frustrating season for me. I've waited eight years to get into another pennant race, then I foul it up by getting completely off form. If I had been pitching close to normal, we'd probably be leading right now."

It sounded as if he was being tough on himself, but unfortunately Mel was right. Although it would have been great to have seen Stottlemyre and Murcer in the World Series or playoffs, it wasn't to be.

Although Mel was erratic that year, he had pitched seven shutouts, which was quite an accomplishment. Remember he had come close to getting a couple more, losing 1–0 in July and being pulled in the last inning for relief help in that eleven inning defeat of Minnesota.

Mel's last full season was 1973, and an early season loss was an indication of the kind of year he was in for. It came in Milwaukee with Stot pitching a no-hitter going into the sixth inning. Darrell Porter broke it up with a single, and Dave May homered for the only two runs and hits the Brewers would get in the game. It was enough, with the Yanks being blanked 2–0. In spite of that loss, Stottlemyre pitched well in the first half, and you'd never have guessed his career was near an end. He won his tenth game on June 30, defeating the Indians on a four-hitter. In his next start, Stot lost a chance to win number eleven. He went into the ninth leading 1–0, but gave up a leadoff hit to Reggie Smith. With lefty Carl Yastrzemski due up next, Houk pulled Mel in favor of lefty Lyle. Yaz promptly singled, pushing Smith to second. When Munson fumbled Orlando Cepeda's sacrifice attempt, it filled the bases. Lyle struck out Rico Petrocelli, but Nettles didn't get rid of a double-play grounder quickly enough, allowing the tying run to score. When Ron Blomberg threw away the ball at the plate, Yaz scored the winning run.

Mel pitched superbly again in his next start, blanking the Twins on July 8 on another four-hitter, his third of the season. Perfectionist Mel wasn't satisfied with his performance. "I actually pitched better against Boston the other day," he stated. "I walked four men and got behind so often. Fortunately, when I needed a good pitch, I was able to throw it."

When Mel pitched another shutout in his next outing against Kansas City, it was his thirty-ninth career shutout and third of the season. He didn't get much print in the papers for his effort though, doing it on the same day Murcer hit three out of the park.

Stot pitched again on July 18, but he lost a tough one to Jim Kaat and the Twins at the Stadium, 3–0. The winning run scored on poor fielding by normally reliable Mel. Rod Carew hit a ball toward the mound and Stottlemyre was slow in reacting to it. A few pitches later, Mel threw the ball away while attempting to pick Carew off at first, and Rod scored a few minutes later on a Bob Darwin hit. It was a tough way to head into the All-Star break and a sign of more difficult times to come.

On August 1 Stot pitched seven and one-third innings at Boston, allowing only two runs; but he was not involved in the decision. In his next start, on August 6 in Detroit, he went into the ninth leading 4–1. With one out and two men on, Houk brought in Lyle again to face lefty swinging Dick McCauliffe. When Nettles bobbled pinch-hitter Al Kaline's double-play grounder, it gave Frank Howard a shot at Sparky. The gentle giant didn't waste the opportunity and hit one into the seats. Stottlemyre was again robbed of what appeared to be a sure victory. "I was wishing Houk would bring Lyle in," Tiger manager Billy Martin said after the game, in his usual outspoken manner. "I kept hoping he'd come in." It was said probably more out of respect for Stottlemyre than disrespect for Lyle.

The woes continued when Mel faced his favorite team, the Angels, at Yankee Stadium in mid-August. He pitched well, as usual, giving up three runs in nine innings, only one of which was earned, thanks to miscues in the infield by Matty Alou, Clarke, and Nettles. The Yanks only managed one run themselves, and Stot took the loss. He had problems the next outing, getting roughed up for five runs in six innings on the artificial surface in Kansas City. It was his eighth straight failure to get number thirteen and his fifth straight loss.

Snakebitten Mel faced ultimate frustration in a gut-wrenching loss to the Athletics. Pitching into the eighth inning, Mel hadn't allowed a run or even a hit against Charlie Finley's soon-to-be-World Champions. With one out, Joe Rudi fisted a looping liner that fell in front of Murcer for the first hit. A sacrifice and a wild pitch later, Stot faced pinch-hitter Vic Davillilo, who singled for the only run of the game. It seemed that no matter what Stottlemyre did, he couldn't pick up victory number thirteen.

After the game, a disgruntled Stottlemyre let it be known he wasn't too happy. "No, there's no consolation in feeling you did a good job," he lamented. "On the bench before the game, I said I'd take a 13–12 victory. It's been so long since I won a game that I'll take anything." Even in frustration Mel was a gentleman, saying nothing about the obvious lack of support from his teammates.

As all good things come to an end, so too do most bad streaks, although the bad ones seem to last longer. Mel's ended on the last day of the worst month of his career, and he beat the Orioles and the tough Jim Palmer 5–2. Even with a three-run lead going into the last inning, Mel wasn't feeling confident, as he told reporters later. "I don't know if I could have survived something happening in the ninth," he remarked. "I'm afraid it would have been more than I could have taken. So many things have happened to me in this stretch that I was ready for anything. When it was all over, I didn't know what to say. It was a strange feeling."

Stottlemyre was asked how the drought had affected him. "I let it get to me after I made four or five attempts," he commented, "but the last two or three starts, I just went out to do the best I could. There was nothing I could do about it, so I stopped letting it upset me."

With the victory, Stot evened his record at 13–13, after he had been 12–7 in mid-July. The win didn't put an end to his bad luck or poor team spirit. In his next outing in Detroit, he went all the way, giving up only two runs, one earned, in a 2–1 loss to the Tigers and Mickey Lolich. In his next game, Mel was bombed by Milwaukee at Yankee Stadium, a game he shouldn't have started. He had a stiff neck but insisted on giving it a shot and succeeded only in picking up his fifteenth loss.

Stottlemyre was back in form when he went up against the division-leading Birds in Baltimore on September 15. He shut them out on a four-hitter for his fortieth, and last, career blanking, leaving him five shutouts behind the all-time Yankee leader in shutouts, Whitey Ford. He pitched well enough to win in his next appearance also, going all the way in a 3–1 loss to the Red Sox and Yankee-killer Luis Tiant. It was Tiant's fourth straight victory over the Bombers that year.

Stottlemyre won his last two starts of the season. He defeated the Indians in Cleveland on September 23, scattering eight hits and allowing one run in going the distance. His last game was a 4–1 victory, evening his record at 16–16.

Mel had felt bad in 1972 for letting his team down. In his mind, he had not pitched well enough and had cost the Yankees a division championship. The number of seasons his teammates let him down, however, denying him numerous chances at winning ball games, was far more. Nineteen seventy-three was a prime example. He needed only four more wins to get his fourth twenty-win season, yet the Yankees must have blown twice that many games for him. His .500 record and 3.07 ERA normally would not impress anyone, but those who followed Stottlemyre that year know that he pitched about as well as he ever had and that his teammates should have been the ones feeling they had let Mel down.

When I heard about Mel Stottlemyre's retirement, it brought back memories of the Mick, Roger, Yogi, Whitey, and Pepi, all of whom played on the 1964 team during Stot's rookie season. It was a club of a far different character than the ones that followed for the next ten years. Mel was the only player remaining from that last pennant-winning team, and his leaving saddened me. Not only was I unsure of whether the Yankees would ever be in the World Series again, Stottlemyre would never have another chance to be in one. No pitcher ever deserved it more than Mel, but fate dealt a tough hand to his baseball career. I only hope the rest of his life has been more rewarding.

I do my best to avoid watching the New York Mets on television, reading about them in the papers, or hearing about them in the news. They're a team that still owns the hearts of most New York baseball fans, despite the lack of tradition and past superstar ball players, which the Yankees have in abundance. Still, two or three times a year, I turn on the Mets broadcast just to try to catch a glimpse of my favorite Yankee hurler. He's disguising himself as a Met pitching coach these days because the Yankee organization failed to hire the man who knows so well the art of pitching and who served them effectively for a decade. It's not a coincidence that the Mets have often had the strongest pitching staff in the majors with Stot as the pitching mentor. Mel leads them with the quiet confidence and control so characteristic of the way he pitched. When he goes to the mound to remind pitchers to stay within themselves, to throw rather than aim but not overthrow, or to throw strikes rather than giving freebies to hitters, it almost looks as if he could take the ball and show them how.

It's amazing the physical condition Stottlemyre has maintained. He almost looks the same as when he was throwing those sinkers to frustrated opponents twenty years ago. Well, not quite the same. He looks different without the Yankee pinstripes.

Thanks for the memories, Mel!

CHAPTER FIVE

ROY WHITE

The Sole Survivor

MY FRIEND STEVE AND I LIKE TO TEST our Yankee trivia knowledge every chance we get.

"Who was the last Yankee to hit four consecutive home runs?" Steve challenged one day, hoping I'd guess Maris, Mantle, Blanchard, or Mattingly.

"Bobby Murcer in June of 1970," I answered haughtily. He should have known better than to ask me a Murcer question. It was my turn.

"Who was the only player on the Yankees to play from 1965 to 1976, when they won the pennant after an eleven-year drought?"

A long pause followed, then Steve replied hesitantly, "Uh, wasn't Stottlemyre on that pennant winner in '76?"

I told him it was Roy White.

"Oh yeah! White. Gee, I should have known that one," Steve admitted.

It wasn't surprising that he hadn't. Many Yankee fans wouldn't. The problem with Roy White was that he was consistently good. Not great. Never great. But always good. With the bat, with the glove, on the

Roy White [National Baseball Library, Cooperstown, New York]

bases. He epitomized the nickname "Mr. Consistency." So reliable was this switch-hitter that he must have been a pleasure for Houk and the skippers who followed to manage. They had only to pencil his name in the lineup and watch him take the field, run down a long fly ball in left, come up with a hit or walk, steal a base, or score a run. He would have his slumps with the bat or a few problems on the field, but they didn't last long. By the end of each year, Roy's stats would be about the same as they always were.

And his effort was always the same: 100 percent. You never caught Roy dogging it on the field, no matter how tough a time he might be having at the plate. He'd always run out grounders or run down fly balls. He'd rarely make mental mistakes on the base paths, such as being picked off first base, which seems so commonplace in today's world of "superior athletes." He'd never complain to the press about lack of playing time, his position in the batting order, or other teammates getting more print in the paper than he did. White was a professional, and you can appreciate his effort and attitude toward the game more now than when he played if you compare the caliber and enthusiasm shown by major leaguers today. How many managers would trade one of their crybaby superstars for a Roy White-type if they could? Probably a lot more than you might imagine.

White played fifteen years for the Yankees, from 1965 to 1979. While other stars such as Tresh, Pepitone, and Murcer were eventually traded away, Roy played his entire career with the Bombers, the only regular of that era, except for Stottlemyre, who could say that. A player's durability is usually a sign of greatness as well, especially at a time when his teammates weren't sticking around too long.

While Roy played briefly in 1965, getting in only fourteen games and forty-two at bats in September at the age of twenty-one, he must have impressed manager Johnny Keane, for he was brought back as a regular at the start of the 1966 campaign. White took advantage of the opportunity. When he homered and singled in a losing cause against the Red Sox at Yankee Stadium on April 25, he raised his average to .375 and had an on-base average of .500. He continued to play well for the next month, but he soon tailed off and batted a mere .225 in 115 games and 316 at bats.

When White's name is mentioned, the first thing that comes to my mind is an incident in late June 1966. The Yankees were trailing the league-leading Orioles 7–5 in the first game of a doubleheader at the Stadium. The Bombers managed to get two men on base in the ninth, and with two outs White came to bat representing the winning run.

Batting left-handed, he lined a drive heading toward the right-field stands. Oriole outfielder Frank Robinson, who won the triple crown and MVP that year, ran back and leaped for the ball, disappearing into the seats. With the ball in the stands, Roy began his home run trot, while Houk charged out of the dugout with right hand extended, ready to congratulate his left-fielder for the game-winning round-tripper. Suddenly, Robinson came out of the stands holding the ball in the air. First-base umpire Hank Soar stopped rotating his index finger signifying a home run and showed a clenched fist instead, signifying an out. Houk changed the direction of his charge and now headed toward Soar. The call stood, and the Yankees lost a ball game to a team they hadn't beaten at home in twelve consecutive tries. Houk protested the game and to reporters afterward

*Does he or doesn't he? That's the question
everyone was asking when Frank Robinson fell
into the stands. Does he have the ball in his
hands or not?* [Photo by Larry Morris/New York
Times]

wailed, "We were robbed out of a ball game! There is
no way any man alive can know if he had the ball
or not when he disappeared from view for fifteen
seconds, then came up with the ball. . . . The rule
should be that if a man catches a ball, falls into
the stands and disappears from view it should be a
home run."

Houk was right, but he lost the protest. "If Baltimore wins the pennant by one game, it will be a

Skipper Ralph Houk argues in vain with umpire Hank Soar over his controversial call that disallowed Roy White's homer. [Photo by Larry Morris/New York Times]

cheap pennant because they never won that game," he said. No one had to worry about that at the end of the year as the Orioles won by a sizable margin.

White wasn't a big home run hitter, but he did hit with power. He hit a career-high twenty-two round-trippers in 1970, the only time he reached the twenty-homer plateau. In seven other seasons, Roy hit double figures in homers, including seventeen in 1968, nineteen in 1971, and eighteen in 1973. He learned early in his career not to become deluded by his occasional long-ball success. In July 1968, after his late home run won a game against the Athletics, White remarked, "I don't care if I hit another home run all season as long as I can hit around .280. . . . I learned my lesson two years ago. I'm still choking up on the bat and swinging to get hits. If they go into the seats that's good, but I'll never be swinging for the fences again."

Although Roy's home runs were limited, many were hit in clutch situations. When Stottlemyre beat soon-to-be thirty-game winner McLain in that 2–1 victory at Yankee Stadium in 1968, it was White who provided Mel with all the runs he needed when he socked a two-run homer. Later in 1968, his two-run blast was the difference in a 3–1 defeat of the Indians in Cleveland. In 1972 when the Yanks were involved in a rare late-season pennant chase, White hit a home run to help defeat Detroit at the Stadium. A few weeks later, his twelfth-inning homer was the game winner in another defeat of the Bengals, this time in Detroit.

White wasn't a big RBI man either, although he could always be counted on to drive in his share. In nine of the ten seasons he played as a regular, White drove in at least fifty runs, including seventy-four in 1969, ninety-four in 1970, and eighty-four in 1971. Roy batted second in the batting order throughout much of his career, depriving him of more opportunities to knock in runs. Houk and managers who followed preferred having him move runners along with bunts or ground balls to the right side, giving the Murcers, Munsons, and Jacksons the chances to bring them home.

White was more impressive as a run scorer. He scored more than 80 runs in six seasons, scoring a career-high 109 in 1970, and a league-leading 104 in 1976. His ability to get on base and run the bases was behind his success. Roy's on-base percentage was always among the best on the ball club. He had a keen eye at the plate and drew an amazing number of base-on-balls for a hitter not known for his power. In five seasons he walked more than eighty times and twice over ninety, leading the league in 1972 with ninety-nine. White often would steal second, leading to his scoring a run, and could always be relied upon to take the extra base when the opportunity arose. He was valuable not only for his speed but for his common sense as well, rarely killing a rally with poor judgment on the base paths.

Above all, however, White was consistent. As Houk correctly predicted in 1968, "Roy should never have a real long slump. He runs so fast that he will beat balls out or bunt if necessary." In fact, in the ten seasons in which Roy collected at least 450 official at bats, he batted below .270 only three times. For three consecutive seasons, from 1969 to 1971, he batted .290, .296, and .292 respectively. From 1967 to 1977 his on-base percentage was below .350 only once. For that same period, Roy failed to hit twenty or more doubles in a season only twice. He kept himself in shape, which allowed him to be among the club leaders in games played for many seasons. He played in each of the 162 games in 1970 and 1973 and played in 155 or more three other times. His military obligations prevented him from playing in more games during some seasons.

Roy's terrible second half in 1966 led to his playing much of the 1967 campaign in the minors. A strong spring training in 1968 changed some minds among Yankee executives, and White found himself as the opening day starter in left field that year. He would become a mainstay at that position for the next ten years. Although he batted only .267, it was high among Yankee starters that season. His seventeen home runs were one fewer than Mantle's club-leading total and more than such power-hitting teammates as Pepitone and Tresh.

White had several outstanding and memorable games in 1968. On June 15 he had a hand in all three Yankee runs in a 3–2 victory over Oakland. White's two-run homer accounted for the first runs of the game. Later, he led off the sixth inning with a single and, showing his savvy on the base paths, tagged up and moved to second when Mantle's fly ball to left carried deeper than expected. His heads-up play proved to be critical when Andy Kosco later singled, allowing Roy to score the deciding run. It was the type of play managers often remember and fans soon forget.

Later that season, the Yankees were playing a doubleheader against the front-running Tigers at Yankee Stadium. Having won the first game, the Bombers went into the eighth inning of the nightcap trailing 3–1. White knotted the contest with a two-out, two-run homer, and it stayed that way for eleven more innings before being called in the nineteenth due to curfew. On September 7 the Yanks tripped the Senators twice, thanks largely to Roy's heroics. He collected two hits in each game, including a double and his sixteenth homer, and he scored six runs, four of them coming in the first game. White continued to plague the Senators when he homered off them the following week, driving in two of the Yanks' four runs.

In the final week of the season, the Yanks found themselves battling the hottest pitcher in the league. No, it wasn't McLain. Boston's Ray Culp went into the game with an 11–1 record since early July, and he showed the Bombers no mercy. He went into the seventh inning with a no-hitter, having allowed only Mantle to reach base on a walk in the fourth. After retiring Jake Gibbs and Mantle, Culp faced White. He explained later why, with the likes of Mantle, Pepitone, Tresh, and Bill Robinson in the lineup, it was White whom he dreaded the most while his no-hitter was intact. "He figured to be the toughest one to shut out. He keeps changing around on you," Culp commented. "Roy is always trying things and will move around in the box and change his style, while other hitters you can get out the same way every time up," something a present-day pitcher might say about Don Mattingly. Culp's fears were well-founded. White lashed a line drive to center for the first and only hit of the game in a 2–0 Yankee loss.

Roy followed up his fine season with a better one in 1969. Although he hit ten fewer home runs, he improved his average by more than twenty points with a .290 mark and raised his RBI total from sixty-two to seventy-four, even though he played in thirty fewer games due to military obligations.

It must have been difficult to shuffle back and forth from reserve duties to baseball, and for White to have played as consistently as he did is to his credit. On July 12, in his first game back after two weeks in the reserves, Roy smacked a pair of hits and drove in a run in a 3–1 Yankee victory over White's patsies, the Senators. The next day, he drove in four of the Yankees' five runs, this time in a losing cause, when the Yanks lost a double-dip to Washington.

White got two more hits against the Senators on July 18, raising his average to .310. He was the only Yankee hitter to be named to the All-Star team in 1969. In his last appearance before the mid-season classic, Roy celebrated his first-time selection by punching out three more hits, putting him among the league leaders in batting.

Roy continued playing like an All-Star. On

August 1 he knocked in two of the Yankees' four runs with a single and a home run in helping the Yanks defeat Marty Pattin and Seattle 4–2. It was a game in which Jim Bouton made an appearance as a reliever against his former teammates. Bouton had been one of my favorite Yankee pitchers. I liked Bouton's mannerisms on the field, especially his hat flying off after almost every pitch. When his book *Ball Four* came out, I stopped liking him. To gain more wealth and fame by disclosing the habits and secrets of your former teammates is hardly admirable. I doubt if Bouton regrets having written the book, but I'm sure many Yankee fans were disappointed with it.

White continued coming through with clutch hits late in the season. On September 6 his RBI single was the only score of the day in a 1–0 triumph over Cleveland. Two weeks later, White picked on the Senators again with two hits, a walk, a stolen base, and a run driven in for a 2–1 nailbiter. The Yankee victory was short and sweet, literally; it was stopped after five innings due to rain. Hank Soar, who had angered Houk and Pepitone earlier in the year, called the game after an hour. He almost ordered play to be resumed when it began to let up, but decided against it. "If we were that lucky all season, we probably would have won the pennant," joked Houk later.

White didn't let up in 1970 and had the best season of his career. His statistics would be enough to impress any owner today. He belted 22 home runs, knocked in 94 runs, collected 180 hits in batting a career-high .296, socked 30 doubles, scored 109 runs, drew 95 bases-on-balls, stole 24 bases, and had a slugging percentage of .473. If credit should be given to one player for the Yanks' second-place finish and 93–69 record in 1970, the best during the eleven years spanning 1965 through 1975, Roy White is the

man who should get it. Not only was his performance on the field effective, but his attitude off the
field helped to inspire some of the younger ball players. The Yankees lost the pennant by a considerable
margin to the powerful Orioles, but they were fun to
watch that year, particularly as they outplayed the
Mets, their cross-town rivals who had won the world
championship in 1969.

Roy continued his outstanding play in 1971, hitting nineteen home runs, driving in eighty-four runs,
and batting .292. Although those stats fell the following year, he hit the ball well throughout; the hits just
didn't fall in. After his homer won a rain-shortened
contest against the Indians in September, White commented, "I was beginning to think I'd never hit another one. The things that have happened to me this
year are unbelievable. I didn't even get mad when
[Alex] Johnson caught that ball. It had become routine." Johnson had robbed Roy of at least a double
and an RBI in his previous at bat with a running,
stretching catch.

It was a tough year for White with the fans as
well. He had a below average throwing arm, and base
runners took liberties when balls were hit to left. The
fans were vociferous in their complaining, often
booing him whenever his throws came in too late or
giving him the familiar "Bronx cheer" on routine
tosses. The criticism was unfair since left field at
Yankee Stadium is one of the most difficult positions
in baseball to cover. Yankee ball players before and
since have had just as much trouble. But the team
hadn't won the pennant in quite awhile, and the fans
were looking for a scapegoat. Roy was frustrated that
he was the victim. After delivering a game-winning
hit against the Indians at the end of June, he told the
press, "This won't ease the noise I get from the fans

out in left field. Every time a runner scores from second, they'll say it is because of my arm. Even if the runner would have scored on any left-fielder, it won't make any difference." White didn't stop there. "No, the stuff that happened . . . hadn't anything to do with me getting the big hit. Getting mad doesn't make me play better. I'd much rather have the fans like me than to be under a magnifying glass where everything I do is magnified."

Houk often took it upon himself to defend his ball players to reporters, and with White it was no exception. "The criticism of Roy is so unfair. There's not a more valuable player on the club [Murcer, Stottlemyre, and Munson were on the team as well], but no one sees anything except his debits. How many extra-base hits does he take away out in left-center? No one thinks of that."

It's true Roy's arm was weaker than most, but Houk's point was well made. Booing a ball player for mental mistakes on the field or for not hustling is understandable, but when a player gives 100 percent, no more can be expected of him. Blaming White for not being able to throw out base runners was about as fair as it would have been to blame Yogi Berra for not running down more fly balls during his tenure in left. Of course, no one booed Yogi.

When White knocked in the winning run against Cleveland, it came in the last inning and made a 1–0 loser out of Gaylord Perry. Considering the hard time most Yankee batters had against the spitballer, White's remarks later were interesting. "Who throws a spitter, Perry?" White asked. "Perry's a sinkerball pitcher. . . . I made up my mind that he wasn't going to psyche me with his reputation for using Vaseline or water on the ball. Perry is very happy when the hitters start worrying about a spitter. In fact, you'll

*Although Roy White was often criticized by fans
for his lack of a strong throwing arm, his adept
fielding more than made up for it. Here he robs
a batter of an extra-base hit with a diving catch.*
[Photo by Larry Morris/New York Times]

note that the more complaining the hitters do, the
easier Perry picks up victories." Murcer should have
paid heed to his teammate's comments.

It's to his credit that White didn't allow some of
the fans' attitude to disrupt his performance or affect
his effort. A month later at Fenway Park, he helped
defeat the Red Sox with his bat and legs. Going into
the sixth inning in a scoreless tie, Murcer doubled
and came in to score the first run on a single by

White. When Sonny Siebert threw wild to first trying to pick him off, Roy dashed to second and moved to third on a ground ball out. With two gone, White dashed home on a 2–1 pitch when he saw Siebert going into a windup. He slid just under the tag of Carlton Fisk, who had to reach up to catch the high, outside fastball. The runs White provided loosened up the other Yanks, and they went on to win by a comfortable margin. "I think that was my third steal of home in the majors," White said. "I did it last year against the White Sox."

The Yanks played 155 games in 1972, and White started in every game. Rizzuto had been the last Yankee to do it, playing all 154 games in 1950. To some fans, it was more important to ride Roy for his less-than-Herculean arm than to give him credit for such a durable feat. Fortunately, many more fans understood his value to the team. I just hope Roy was aware of that "Silent Majority."

White got off to a miserable start in 1973, again due in part to his hitting the ball where the defenders were. When he broke out of a slump at the end of June with three hits, including two doubles, in a game against Cleveland, he remarked, "I guess that line drive was caught just to prove to me that things haven't changed completely." Roy was talking about a ball Chris Chambliss, then an Indian, snared with a leap and turned into a double play.

He continued to rebound with the stick, smacking four hits, including two triples and a home run, while knocking in four runs in a doubleheader sweep of the Indians a couple of days later. They were White's first triples in more than two years. The following week, the Twins were a victim of Roy's power surge when he connected for a two-run homer, helping the Yanks pull out a victory. On July 20 he smacked three more hits, including a double and a grand slam home run, driving in seven runs in a pair of victories against the White Sox at Yankee Stadium.

On August 13 White hit homers from both sides of the plate for the second time in his career. When he was advised that only three other players had done it more times, Roy seemed surprised. "That's unbelievable," he said. "You'd think a lot more guys would have done it."

I remember that game more for the great catch he made in left than for his hitting heroics. With two outs in the sixth, Bob Oliver hit a ball toward the left-field wall, and White made a leaning, one-handed catch to rob him of a two-run homer and save the shutout for Doc Medich. "I thought I had a shot at it when he hit it," White admitted. "But I began to doubt it the last couple of feet. I knew it would depend on how I hit the barrier. Then I got one foot up on the railing and managed to grab it standing on one foot."

Unfortunately, Roy's hitting streaks were not long-lasting, and productive games were few and far between for most of 1973. His average of .246 was the lowest of his career as a regular, and although he racked up eighteen homers, he struck out a career-high eighty-one times, not what a manager expects from his second-place hitter. Yet, despite his struggles at the plate, he continued his effort on the field. In September he prevented Earl Williams from tying the game for the Orioles with another leaping catch over the wall.

The frustration White experienced in 1973 came to a head on August 25 in a game against the A's. In the first inning, Bert Campaneris hit a drive to left that White caught, then dropped. Umpire Jim Odom ruled the ball to be in play, prompting White to charge in his direction. Roy thought he had held onto the ball long enough. After arguing too long and too vehemently, he was tossed from the game for the first time in his career.

White went on to play several more years for the Yanks. He was fortunate to be on the pennant-winning team of 1976 and the World Championship teams of '77 and '78. Roy must have felt immense satisfaction during the clubhouse celebrations of those years. To have been with the team for so long, wondering if he would ever be involved in post-season play, and then finally to be a part of it—the thrill was Roy's to savor. Munson, Nettles, Chambliss, and the others had come in the seventies, and their frustration was limited to a mere half-a-dozen years or less. White played a dozen long years in pinstripes before experiencing what had been a tradition throughout Yankee history.

And no other player deserved it more. White was the perfect role model for kids. He gave his best on the field, handled himself like a gentleman off-field, was respected and appreciated by his managers, and was well-liked and admired by his peers. He didn't use his minority heritage as an excuse to complain to reporters about his status on the team or that he didn't get as much ink as some of his teammates. Roy would leave that kind of talk for other "stars." It wasn't his style.

Unfortunately, the sports world offers little these days in terms of role models for kids: an owner who would resort to trickery and bribery and another who blurts out bigoted remarks; players who complain that their salaries are not enough, when their efforts on the field are worth much less; athletes who commit crimes of rape and sexual abuse; players who complain about their lack of recognition and point to their ethnic makeup as an excuse; players who use illegal drugs, only to be given two, three, or even seven chances instead of being kicked out of the game after the first offense. With such role models in the sports world these days, it's a wonder youth haven't become corrupted by their influence. Or maybe they have.

Baseball isn't just a game. It's part of Americana. Whether they know or like it, the players are part of this country's psyche. When a player like White leaves the game, it's such a loss, not only because of what he meant to the Yankees and to baseball, but because there are so few like him taking his place. Largely gone are the days of the humble ball player who gives his all on the field and handles himself responsibly off, who cares about what he puts into the game, not just what he gets out of it, and who sets a good example for ever-watchful youngsters. Roy White types are going the way of the dinosaurs, and when their extinction is realized, we'll have a baseball world filled with players who care more about their agents' instructions than their managers'.

The kids will be watching and imitating. When they go to school, they won't have to listen to their teachers, because their favorite players don't have to listen to their managers. When they have a disagreement, they'll use their fists because that's how their favorite ball players solve their problems. And it'll be all right to use drugs, because their favorite ball players used them, and they still look healthy and successful.

And when they grow up, they'll be remembering their "heroes" not for the steals of home, or clutch home runs, or diving catches, but for how much money they made or how controversial they were. And if I'm still alive and I tell them about Roy White and try to explain how important he was to the Yankees, they'll probably laugh and say, "Hell! He never made five million dollars in one year. How good could he have been?"

Well, at least my generation will remember and understand.

Thanks for the memories, Roy!

Thurman Munson [National Baseball Library, Cooperstown, New York]

CHAPTER SIX

THURMAN MUNSON

Fallen Hero

IT'S BEEN SAID THAT MOST CATCHERS don't have looks on their side. When Thurman Munson played his first full season with the Yankees in 1970, I didn't like him. He was too ugly to like. With his rotund yet stocky build and his thick Fu Manchu mustache, he looked more like a walrus from a Woody Woodpecker cartoon than a prospective Yankee hero.

Munson always looked so serious. His appearance and personality were not conducive to his being liked immediately, and he always looked so disheveled. A ball game would rarely end without Thurm dirtying his uniform or having his hair mussed up. His face never looked clean-shaven, and his pictures in the paper looked like they were taken from the wall of a post office.

The way he played the game, however, soon changed my mind. He not only wanted to win, he expected to. When asked if the Yankees could catch the high-flying Orioles in midseason of 1970, Munson replied confidently, "Sure we can take them, why not? That's what we're getting paid for, isn't it?" Pretty cocky for a rookie.

Thurman earned his pay. No one in the game during his time played any harder. He guarded the plate against would-be scorers as tenaciously as a lioness guards her cubs. He broke up double plays with a vengeance, sending unwary shortstops and second basemen limping to the dugout. Munson didn't look as if could run well, but he could, often outrunning slow bouncers to the left side. He overcame the extra steps needed to reach first from the right-handed batter's box by leaving it with a catlike quickness as soon as the ball was hit.

He used that quickness to even greater advantage when playing defense. Thurman was the best at getting to slow rollers, spinning, and throwing out base runners at first. He had a quick-release throw that he perfected after experience had taught him to control it, nailing an impressive number of rabbits sprinting to second. He caught more than his share of sleepyhead runners at first with unexpected throws from behind the rear ends of southpaw swingers. He startled quite a few unwary opponents at second as well.

In July 1973 the Yanks played their last game before the All-Star break. Leading by a run in the final frame, Fritz Peterson allowed the first two White Sox batters to reach base. Pinch-runner Joe Keough lingered too far away from second and learned the hard way not to do that against Mr. Munson. Before Keough knew it, he was being tagged out on a surprise throw by Thurman, and with the pressure off, Lyle got the last two outs for the Yanks' victory.

Except for Mantle, I never saw a Yankee who was as good a clutch hitter as Munson. Time and again he

Munson makes a desperate dive for Fred Patek of the Royals during playoff action in 1977. Thurman never lacked hustle whether he was fielding at backstop or running the bases. [AP/Wide World Photos]

would come through with game-tying and winning hits after his teammates had failed to do so. Reggie Jackson had us believing it was his straw doing the stirring with his October magic, but there would never have been any October to talk about in '77 and '78 if it hadn't been for Munson's bat in August and September. While Reggie was striking out, Thurman was delivering. That some of the press and fans fell for Jackson's lines upset Munson, but his teammates knew better.

In his first three games in August 1969, Munson quickly showed what he was made of. Playing in a scoreless tie in his first major league start, Thurm delivered a clutch hit in the seventh inning, allowing the go-ahead run to move to third while he alertly went to second. He added a two-run single in the eighth, cementing a 5–0 defeat over Reggie Jackson's A's. He also took charge behind the plate, calling the shots sometimes over the objections of veteran Yankee hurler Al Downing. "Yes, I called the game," the rookie readily admitted afterward. "We had a few disagreements in the early innings, then we got along great." That meant Al started seeing things Thurman's way. It was Downing's first shutout in over two years.

A rookie's first hit would usually be a big thrill, but Munson revealed he was thinking about something else when he saw his hit dropping in the outfield. "I wasn't really thinking it was my first major league hit," he said. "I was just hoping it went somewhere to get Gene [Michael] to third. After all, it was a scoreless game. If there had been no one on base, it might have hit me more." A team player would think that way.

In his next start two days later, Munson had another first in the majors—a home run, coming off the right-hander Lew Krausse that helped to defeat the A's for the third straight game. The homer was a noteworthy one, as were many of Thurman's blasts, this one coming in the middle of three consecutive round-trippers. Murcer had hit one to lead off the sixth, and unlikely fence reacher Gene Michael followed Munson's shot. It had been nineteen years since the last Yankee trio—Richardson, Mantle, and Pepitone—had hit three in a row. Reading Thurm's comments in the paper the next day, you'd think he felt more relieved than excited. "It felt good to get the first one so quickly. Now I don't have to think about it," he said.

In Munson's third game as a Yankee a couple of

Munson walks away from the action at home plate during the 1977 season. Many felt that Thurman, not Reggie Jackson, was the key player on the championship teams of the seventies. [AP/Wide World Photos]

days later, Twins batter John Roseboro hit a squibbler a few yards toward third. Thurm jumped out of his squat position, picked the ball up while turning and firing to first in almost one motion, and made an out on what looked like a sure hit. In the seventh he blew away the same Roseboro trying to steal second. The aging Roseboro was past his prime and his base-stealing attempts were minimal that year, but he must have wanted to test the young catcher who had robbed him in his last at bat. It wasn't even close. In the bottom half of the inning, Munson fell behind at the plate 0–2 against veteran Al Worthington with the bases loaded. But Munson won the battle, working out a base-on-balls to drive in the go-ahead and eventual winning run.

Throughout his career, Thurman took charge. He was the leader. As Stottlemyre described him once in the early seventies, "He's the boss. Frankly, sometimes he scares me." For Mel to make that statement exemplifies the respect Munson earned from his teammates.

If Thurman scared Stottlemyre, it wasn't to the same degree that he intimidated the opposition, with zeal and passion for winning that were uniquely his. Long-time major leaguer Gene Woodling, who scouted Munson in 1968, remarked, "I never saw a young guy with more competitive spirit. He'll battle right down the line and never quit." Even his wife, Diane, admitted once, "He even likes to beat me in Ping-Pong."

He showed that fire in a late-season game against the Indians in 1972. With the game tied at three apiece and one out in the eleventh, Munson got his third hit of the game. In an attempted hit-and-run play, Gene Michael took the pitch instead of swinging, leaving Thurman running into a sure tag and out at second. He went into shortstop Frank Duffy hard and heavy, and the ball went flying toward the outfield, allowing Munson to go to third. Michael then grounded to the drawn-in Duffy, and again Munson looked like an out when he charged home. Still reeling from his meeting with Munson, Duffy fumbled the ball and threw wild to the plate, allowing the winning run to score. "I knew I was dead," Munson explained about his run-in with Duffy. "I knew all I could do was try to knock the ball out of his hand. I got him with my shoulder, and it worked out all right."

Thurman's best remembered heroics came during the team's pennant-winning years, but he had been coming up with clutch hits long before then. In his first full season, he won rookie-of-the-year honors with a .302 batting average in 132 games played. Although his numbers looked mediocre the next two seasons, Munson contributed his share of important and timely hits. He won a game against the Indians in July 1972 with a tie-breaking single. A week later, his home run was the game winner in a 4–1 win over Oakland. Horace Clarke had been hit with a pitch prior to Thurman's blast. It was not the only time Munson made opposing pitchers pay for hitting his teammates with errant deliveries. In 1973, in a game against the Tigers, Lolich nailed Murcer on the right arm with a fastball that forced Bobby out of the game. Munson came to the plate and nailed another Lolich fastball into the Tiger Stadium left-field seats.

Nineteen seventy-three was one of Thurman's best years—some might argue it was his best. He hit a career-high twenty homers and twenty-nine doubles, and knocked in seventy-four runs, batting sixth or seventh in the order most of the season. He scored eighty runs, just five short of his career high in 1977. He batted .301 but had a career-high slugging percentage of .487. His on-base percentage of .364 was topped only in 1975 with a .372 mark, and his forty-eight walks were more than in any other following season.

Unlike other stars who ran up good numbers at unimportant times during ball games, Thurman always had his share of big hits, and 1973 was no exception. On July 8 he broke open a tight ball game in the sixth inning with his twelfth home run of the season, helping to defeat the Twins on the road. When Minnesota came to town the following week,

Munson's thirteenth homer late in the game provided Pat Dobson with an important insurance run in gaining a victory in the second game of a twin bill. Thurman had sat out the first game with a bruised chest, and replacement Gerry Moses starred by driving in the winning run. When reporters brought up Moses' contribution afterward, Munson expressed mock concern saying, "I hope I don't turn out to be another Wally Pipp," referring to the man Lou Gehrig replaced at first base one day, never to relinquish the job.

Munson was selected to play in the All-Star game that year. Soon afterward, in a game against Milwaukee, he faced Jim Colburn, his former teammate on the American League squad. Colburn related after the game how he had been riding Thurman on the bench during the mid-season classic, making fun of his ability and threatening to challenge him at the plate in every meeting between them. "I guess he had the last laugh on that one," Colburn admitted. He was referring to Munson's getting four hits off him, including a game-winning single in the twelfth inning, pinning a 1–0 loss on the Brewer hurler and dropping his record to 13–6.

An unusually relaxed Thurman talked to reporters after the game. When someone mentioned that to him he replied, "You fellows are just getting to know me better. Maybe I have a strange sense of humor or something, but we haven't had our lines of communication open too good." Both Munson and the press were probably to blame for that throughout his career. The temperamental catcher often refused to talk to the press and could be rude and insulting at times. But his attitude may have been induced by irresponsible reporters who frequently misquoted him or used his words out of context. Thurman may have resolved not to speak with them because he thought that might be the best way to avoid trouble and aggravation. If the public has a right to the best possible sports coverage, as the press is quick to proclaim when athletes resist interrogation, reporters shouldn't forget their duty to report fairly and honestly. Otherwise they should expect—and probably deserve—reactions similar to Munson's.

On July 27 Thurman had a big game against the Brewers. He had three hits, scored two runs, and drove in another in a 7–6 squeaker at Yankee Stadium. With the Yanks still thinking pennant, he explained the reason for his recent surge, which had him batting .445 over the previous fourteen games. "I think being in the battle for the pennant helps me," he said. "I love the competition, and it makes the adrenaline flow a little faster. You stop thinking of your own stats and think only of the whole picture. My one aim now is to do something to win a ball game."

The catcher continued to sizzle in early August, hitting a two-run homer in a losing cause against the Tigers. On August 8 the Yanks faced Texas at Yankee Stadium and were trailing 2–1 in the final frame. Murcer led off with a double, and after Jim Hart failed to advance him, Munson ripped a single to center, tying the score. With two outs and Thurman now on second, Michael looped a hit to right and Munson challenged the strong arm of Bill Sudakis. His gamble won the game for the Yanks. "I didn't know where the ball was," explained Munson. "All I knew is Gene had hit it and there were two out, so what could happen if I kept going? We just had to pull one out like that."

Two days later, Thurman starred in a slugfest against the A's. When Jackson rocked Lindy McDaniel for a pair of home runs, Munson matched him by getting two hits, four RBIs, and his sixteenth four-bagger. Later in August, he hit number seventeen off the Angels' Clyde Wright late in the game, accounting for the team's only runs.

The next day, he faced California's Nolan Ryan. Ryan could be the greatest pitcher who ever lived; certainly he's the most durable. He's struck out many more batters than his closest competitors and has more no-hitters (seven) than anyone else. Just as amazing are the dozen one-hitters he's thrown. His nineteen low-hitters are a major league record that will likely never be equaled.

When Ryan, who already had 300 strikeouts for the season, faced the Yankees in Anaheim that day, the home crowd was filled with excitement in anticipation of Ryan's performance. And when Munson blooped a hit to center with one out in the first inning, many in the crowd must have been disappointed slightly, realizing their chance to see a no-hitter had quickly vanished. How much more disheartened they must have been when the game ended with Munson's hit still the only one on the board for the Bombers. Their hero had just missed putting another notch on his pitching belt. Munson, in character, showed little sympathy for Ryan after the game. "No, I'm not sorry it was a cheap hit," he blurted to reporters. "I tried to bunt in the ninth for a second hit." Whether dealing with a rookie or veteran star, Munson treated all opponents with equal disrespect on the playing field.

When the Yanks lost to front-running Baltimore in September, Munson's eighteenth homer was wasted. A couple of days later, Thurman took Joe Coleman deep twice, driving in three of the Yanks' four runs in a 4–3 victory in Detroit. He had tried unsuccessfully to bunt with the tying run on in the eighth before connecting for his second of the game and twentieth of the season. "It wasn't a dumb play," Thurman said in defending himself later. "I wanted to get the tying run to second. After Roy stole second, I just wanted to get a base hit to get him home."

When the Yanks went into Boston on September 18, Munson entered the contest with a .299 average and was battling Murcer for the club lead. Facing Bill Lee, 16–8 at the time, Thurman punched out four singles in four appearances at the plate, but his teammates could only manage three more on their way to a 4–2 defeat. With his team now out of the pennant race, the catcher was looking for other ways to stay motivated. "I'd be lying if I said I didn't want to lead the club in hitting," he said. "I'd like to see Bobby hit .350, but then I'd want to hit .351. I was tickled to get the hits."

That the Bombers lost the pennant that year wasn't Munson's fault. Rather, erratic pitching and mental mistakes during the important late-season games were the chief causes. The loser mentality was still etched in the minds of many veteran players, and it showed on the field and off, as they frequently blamed bad bounces and bad breaks for their losses during post-game interviews. It would take a couple more years before Munson's "We're better than they are" philosophy would replace the old one around the clubhouse.

Thurman's sense of pride in being the best at what he did was a major reason why he excelled. When Boston's Carlton Fisk beat him out in the All-Star vote in 1973 by half a million votes, it may have inspired him to have the outstanding second half that he did. He was hurt knowing that the fans around the league preferred Fisk over him, but it should have been easy for him to understand. In contrast to pudgy Munson, Carlton was tall and good-looking, with facial features, including an ever-present stoic look, that gave him the appearance of a Roman god. Unlike Munson, Fisk was a home run hitter, roles which almost certainly would have been reversed had they switched home ball parks. The players around the league understood Munson's value, but for Thurman it wasn't enough. Fisk was his rival, and that made him an enemy.

Fisk's arrogance earned him a negative reputation around the league, one that may have been deserved, but he had a desire to win and a competitiveness comparable to Munson's. In a game at the end of July, Boston trailed by a run in the ninth and the Yanks were making a bid for an insurance run. With White on third and one out, Ron Blomberg lifted a medium fly ball to left that looked as if it would bring Roy home easily. As White approached the plate standing up, Fisk stood there playing possum. He prevented White from touching the plate, spiking him in the process, while grabbing the throw from the outfield and tagging him out. It was the kind of play Yankee fans hated but Red Sox fans adored Fisk for. It didn't make Carlton any more popular with the Yankee team either. "I knew there would be no play, so I didn't try to knock him down," an annoyed White complained. "As I stepped for the plate, he lifted his foot and jarred me off base. I knew I hadn't touched the plate, but there was nothing I could do but remember."

The episode added fuel to an already fired-up feud between Munson and Fisk. "I'm surprised a big All-Star catcher would have to resort to tactics like that," chided Munson, who couldn't resist a stab at his rival. He also left a warning that there might be an aftermath to what had taken place, saying, "I wish he'd pull it on someone his size. He sure made sure he had the edge this time."

Yankees and Red Sox players traditionally don't need any additional motivation when playing each other, but the Fisk incident along with the closeness of the pennant race at the time made the game between the two clubs the next day even more intense. When Munson wound up on third base in a tie game with one out in the ninth, the stage was set for the inevitable confrontation. Perhaps sensing Munson's eagerness to meet Fisk close up, Houk called for a suicide squeeze. Hitter Gene Michael played his part in setting up the "Clash of the Titans" by missing the bunt attempt, bringing a charging Munson barreling into Fisk, who had thrown Gene out of the way and was bracing himself. It was the classic example of the irresistible force meeting the immovable object. The result was a victory for both, in a way. Munson was flipped over and tagged out by the gutsy Fisk, but his wrestling tactics inspired a boxing exhibition from Munson—and then Michael. Thurman's fist found Fisk's face, and when Carlton's teammates rushed to hold back Munson, Michael showed his pugilistic expertise by throwing some jabs at the beleaguered Red Sox backstop.

After the game, the three combatants and the "referee" all had some interesting comments. Said Michael, "After missing the bunt, I couldn't get out of the way. Fisk came out so fast, then he pushed me and I rolled to the side as Thurman hit him. It was a good fight."

Home plate umpire Nestor Chylak explained why he had ejected Fisk and Munson from the game but not Michael. "When those things explode it's like a three-ring circus . . . and you don't know what's going on. In this case, we ejected the two catchers since they started it. Then you get the game going again."

Fisk seemed more interested in dispelling the idea that he had been the loser of the "Bedlam in Beantown" by claiming, "Munson didn't lay a hand on me [Red Sox manager Eddie Kasko and Chylak confirmed that Munson had punched him]. Michael got me from the blind side." Fisk then spoke in a more conciliatory manner. "I don't know if there will be a carryover or not. Guess we'll have to see. I have no feud with Munson except that I try to play better than he does, just as he tries to play better than I do."

Predictably, Munson was less diplomatic, speaking in victorious tones despite the Yankees' having lost the game. "How did he look?" Thurm asked, gloating like a kid having won a fight in the schoolyard. "I got him in the left eye, which is why I got thrown out of the game. No, I didn't get mad because of the collision. That's all part of the game. I got mad because he flipped me with his legs after the play was over."

Whether or not Munson would have reacted as violently to any other catcher is debatable. But his intimidating remarks the day before make one think Munson may have wanted an excuse to take a poke at Fisk. That Thurman still harbored a grudge was evident when he said after the fight, "I don't think any less of Fisk now than I did before, and you know what I thought of him before." When Thurman didn't like you, at least he let you know it.

People sometimes try to remember where they were and what they were doing years after a tragic event. I was in my high school English class when an announcement was made over the loudspeaker that

President Kennedy had been shot. In 1968 I was watching television in my parents' living room when regular broadcasting was interrupted to inform viewers of the Bobby Kennedy shooting. On March 30, 1980, the morning following the most exciting night of my life, I was with my wife in a Binghamton hospital room with my eight-hour-old daughter Jackie when we heard about the assassination attempt on President Reagan.

In early August 1979 my bride-to-be, Lola, and I were visiting friends on Staten Island, New York. Larry, an old college chum, and I were debating why the Yankees weren't doing well in the pennant race and what their prospects were for turning things around when the phone rang. It was my brother Gene. He told me that Munson had been killed when his plane burned while flying home. My first thoughts were how sad it would be watching the Yanks without No. 15, the captain, behind the plate. Then I wondered if the Yanks would ever win another world championship without the skills and leadership of Thurman. As of this writing they haven't.

Thurman's family was precious to him, and it is sadly ironic that he had learned to fly a plane to enable himself to be with his family in Canton, Ohio, more often. O. Henry couldn't have come up with a more tragic conclusion.

Shortly after the tragedy, there were demands by fans to have Munson inducted into the Hall of Fame. The normal procedure is to wait five years after a player's retirement before accepting his nomination as a candidate for Cooperstown. Many didn't want to wait. The sudden departure of their hero inspired them to seek immediate honors for him. Why delay the inevitable? they protested.

I wasn't one of them, though not because I didn't

*The distraught family of the late catcher Thurman Munson
at funeral services in Canton, Ohio, on August 7, 1979.
Munson was killed in a plane crash a few days earlier.
[AP/Wide World Photos]*

like Munson or felt that he didn't belong in the Hall.
I thought that by electing him right away, critics later
might argue that Munson made it because of his
tragic death, not on his achievements. I wanted to see
Thurman make it on his own, and when he was
elected in five years, everyone would realize he be-
longed there.

It's been more than a dozen years since then, and
I'm still waiting for the selection committee to do
what they should have done years ago. Why haven't

they acted? It's true that time heals all wounds, but it shouldn't make us forget either. We shouldn't forget the greatness that was Thurman Munson. We shouldn't forget the hustling, the clutch hitting, the superb defense, the fiery leadership, and the inspiration. We shouldn't forget the lifetime .292 batting average (six points less than Mickey Mantle's) or the five seasons he batted over .300, missing a sixth by only six points. We shouldn't forget the three straight seasons of 100 RBIs or more, a feat accomplished by few Yankee players (Mickey never did it two seasons in a row). We shouldn't forget that he accomplished all this by the age of thirty-two, an age many baseball experts would say is the prime of a player's career, and that the chance to improve on those statistics was taken away from Munson.

The playing career of Roy Campanella, the great Dodger, was also shortened when he was permanently injured in an accident. The Hall of Fame committee sent Roy to Cooperstown. He belongs there. His accomplishments were exceptional and would have been greater had he continued playing. Fortunately, Roy wasn't killed. We could still see him once in a while and remember the greatness that was once his and the wonderful memories that he gave us. Had he not been elected, could we have looked upon him as he smiled bravely in his wheelchair, throwing out the first pitch or accepting the honors bestowed on him, without protesting that he wasn't in the Hall of Fame? And our complaints would have been justified, for it would have been an injustice to overlook Roy.

The expression "Out of sight, out of mind" is sad but true. Thurman's gone, so it's up to us to remember. It's up to us to remind others. It's up to us to keep complaining and protesting to the press, the

Yankee organization, the commissioner, and to anyone we feel needs reminding that what belongs to
Thurman still is being denied.

In eulogizing Munson, Bobby Murcer said:

> The life of a soul on Earth lasts longer than his depar-
> ture. He lives on in your life and the life of all others
> who knew him. . . . He was No. 15 on the field and
> he will be No. 15 at the doors of Cooperstown.

Let's not allow Bobby's sentiments to be proven
wrong.

When Thurman died, we felt sad for ourselves as
much as for him. He would no longer be part of our
world. But we still have our memories of him and
what he accomplished. That's a helluva lot!

Thanks for the memories, Thurman!

CHAPTER SEVEN

HONORABLE MENTION

ALTHOUGH THEY WEREN'T MY FAVOR-
ite ball players and I followed their careers with
casual interest, there were some Yankees who left me
with good memories during those unsuccessful seasons, and not mentioning them in this book would
be an injustice.

Sparky Lyle
    A tobacco-chewing practical joker, Sparky looked
and acted about as sophisticated as Jed Clampett.
The tune "Pomp and Circumstance" would seem out
of place at a ball game, but how much more absurd it
was when used as Lyle's theme song before each of
his relief entrances at Yankee Stadium. Organist Eddie Layton must have chuckled once or twice thinking how a song normally reserved for presidents and
royalty could be used for wise guy Sparky.
    Considering how important and valuable Lyle
was to the Yanks of the early to mid-seventies, the
song was indeed appropriate. Sparky's slider brought
with it many an out and saved many games. Hitters,
watching balls heading for the plate belt high, would
wind up swinging at balls in the dirt. As exaggerated

as that may sound, that's how good Lyle's slider was. Many still say that when he had it working the way he wanted, it was the best.

I recall several of his outstanding efforts. Once the Yanks were in Minnesota and Stottlemyre pitched into the eleventh inning before the Yanks scored. With a 1–0 lead, Mel gave up a leadoff hit. Out came Houk and in came Sparky, who finished off the Twins one-two-three, striking out the last two batters. At the end of August 1972, Lyle notched his twenty-ninth save of the season, tying the club record at that time, set by Lindy McDaniel and Luis Arroyo. He went on to break the record, since surpassed by Dave Righetti. After the game, Lyle's disregard of records became apparent. Said Sparky, "Hell, I don't pay any attention to records. My only concern is that I do my job, not how many records are set."

Later in September, Sparky's thirty-fourth save equaled the American League mark at the time, but again Lyle didn't seem to care. "You mean they didn't play my song?" he joked about Layton not ushering him in properly. "I didn't miss it."

Mike Kekich, a Yankee for a few seasons, explained once how he and the other starters felt about having Lyle around. "With that guy out there, why should Ralph take a gamble on anyone?" he asked. "Hell, I think they keep that car heated up from the fifth inning on. I'll tell you one thing, however, and that is this—it's a great comfort to know he's out there."

Houk used Lyle often, some might have thought too often. But Lyle loved it. If he had a bad outing, he would never use the excuse that he was too tired. In fact, if he had not pitched for several days, at times Sparky would have problems with being too strong, and his slider would not react normally. He once claimed to be able to judge before a game whether his slider would do the job. "As soon as I pick up the ball, if the ball feels good to me . . . I know I'm all right."

Those times were more frequent than not. His teammates knew that in pressure situations they could count on "The Count."

Graig Nettles

After Clete Boyer's departure, the Yankees began a search for a reliable third baseman. It ended when they picked up Graig Nettles. Nettles came from the Indians in the early seventies and brought with him a potent bat, a steady and sometimes spectacular glove, and a ready quip. The master of the one-liner, Graig could be outspoken, directing sarcastic remarks toward owner, teammates, and fans. He was always honest though, and other players enjoyed his humor in the clubhouse.

Usually sure-handed, during the first couple of years Nettles had his share of problems at third. Part of it may have been playing in the Big Apple. Yankee fans cheer like no others when they're pleased with a player's performance, but they can also be demanding and unsupportive when things aren't going well. When Nettles's errors became too frequent, so did the booing. When he hit his seventeenth homer of the season in August 1973, Graig's acid tongue went to work later. "I was waving to my fans, both of them," he mocked in explaining why he had gestured toward the box seats after his round-tripper. "New York fans aren't good baseball fans because they boo the club when it's going badly. It affects me psychologically, and it hurts. We're all trying to do our best, but the fans expect perfection." Nettles wasn't finished. "Errors are part of the game, but the fans don't under-

stand that. Only the bad players don't make errors,"
meaning that their range and aggressiveness in fielding ground balls is not as good. When Graig's fielding
plays highlighted the 1977 and 1978 World Series,
Yankee fans must have wondered how they could
ever have booed such a showman.

Tom Tresh

Although he had a few good seasons with the
Yanks, Tresh never reached the star status some expected of him. What I remember most about him was
his constantly changing his batting stance. Thinking
too much at the plate may have prevented him from
swinging naturally, prolonging instead of shortening
his slumps. The pressure of following in Mantle's
footsteps (like Mantle, he was a switch-hitting outfielder with power) may have been too much as well.
Murcer handled it better because he understood his
limitations. Tresh's expectations may have been un-
realistically high. Still, he put in eight solid years
with the Yanks, including a monster home run in the
1964 World Series.

Rocky Colavito

Colavito is known as one of baseball's greatest
sluggers. He hit them out with consistency while
playing for the Indians and Tigers. He played briefly
for the Yanks in 1968, and although he wasn't the
threat that he used to be at the plate, I remember a
game when Houk brought him in to pitch. The Yanks
were trailing badly, so Houk decided to give his bullpen a rest by using the Rock, who pitched almost
three innings of shutout ball. In the meantime, the
Yanks rallied for five runs and went on to win. It was
Rocky's first victory and only decision as a professional pitcher in the big leagues. When a reporter

asked Houk if he were raising the surrender flag by bringing Colavito in, Ralph retorted, "That's ridiculous! Rocky has pitched before and can throw. I guess he proved it, didn't he?"

As a matter of fact, in his only other pitching performance, Colavito also allowed no runs in three innings when he pitched against the Tigers in 1958. That leaves him with an impressive lifetime ERA of 0.00 and a won–lost percentage of 1.000.

Ralph Houk

Casey Stengel was a showman and a treat to watch. Yogi Berra was, too, besides having luck on his side. No one could match the spirit and desire to win that Billy Martin had, and Bob Lemon seemed to have the perfect personality for that 1978 Yankee team. There were Gene Michael, Lou Piniella, Dallas Green, Bucky Dent, Stump Merrill, and now Buck Showalter all taking turns managing during impatient George's reign as owner. Oh, yes, there was Ralph Houk.

No one ever had anything unkind to say about Houk when he managed those pennant-winning teams of the early sixties. When he took over for Keane in 1966, and the team responded briefly with a winning streak, Ralph was given credit for their efforts. At the end of the season, when the team failed and followed that with losing season after losing season, the fans and some of the press soured on Houk. Naturally, he was to blame for the Yankees' downfall. When Steinbrenner took charge, he wasted little time in getting rid of the Major.

But I've never read anything said by anyone who played under Houk that was critical of him. He was

Ralph Houk in the Yankee Stadium in his first appearance there after replacing Johnny Keane as manager in the spring of 1966. [Photo by Barton Silverman/New York Times]

respected and liked because he stood by his men. Rather than protesting in public about players' mistakes on the field, Houk reserved his criticisms for private discussion. He preferred to talk with his players face to face rather than having them read or hear about it somewhere else. As a result, he got the most possible out of the teams he managed.

Fans are always looking for someone to blame, and the manager usually hears it first. In spite of all the criticism fans laid on Steinbrenner during his final days prior to his banishment, they loved it when he ran the show because he was so quick to hire and fire. At the beginning his approach worked since the team was talented enough to win anyway. However, when the stars got too old, were traded, or became free agents and couldn't wait to leave, the Yankees started losing again. And when his tactics of switching managers stopped working, he became the primary target of the fans.

I liked Billy Martin, but I would have preferred having Houk at the helm in 1976 when the Yanks won their first pennant in eleven years. With Guidry, Lyle, Munson, Chambliss, White, and Randolph, they would have won with Ralph, too. After being with the team while they were losing, Houk deserved to be there when they won.

Martin was colorful, but so was Houk. Who could forget those big, long cigars he used to smoke, the tobacco juice he used to spit while standing at the edge of the dugout, one foot on the second step? He'd grab a handful of dirt and pebbles every so often as a nervous habit, and he'd be the first to congratulate any Yankee who had just hit a home run. And no manager could get himself kicked out of a game in more splendid fashion than the Major—going face to face with the umpire, taking off his cap, revealing his full head of brown hair, raising his arms in disgust, and kicking dirt a mile high with his right foot (never at the umpire though). Martin would deliberately try to show up the ump as much as he could, but Houk's tantrums were well-controlled, almost rehearsed, and there was just so much he would allow himself to do on the field. What a treat it would be at a Yankee game to see Ralph put on his show.

Jim Ogle, a noted sportswriter, wrote in 1968 that he felt Houk deserved to be named manager of the year in spite of the team's fifth-place showing. "With the baseball season in its last quarter, the Yankees still have a chance to finish in the money. To one watching the ball club day in and day out, the high estate of the club is a great tribute to the management skills of Houk. The current Yankee club will never be remembered when the roll is called of great Yankee teams. Putting it bluntly, it is a very ordinary club with a lot of flaws. It is last in the majors in hitting, ranks ninth in the league in scoring, has a very ordinary defense, and yet is battling for a piece of the money."

Ogle was right. Houk was a great manager, and he would have been recognized as such if he hadn't begun with such great teams, had such poor ones afterward, and been denied the opportunity to manage the team for a few more seasons. He was a "Major" reason why I kept following the Yankees.

Thanks for the memories, gentlemen!

CONCLUSION

I WAS LYING ON THE COUCH IN MY LIVing room watching the Yanks. They were treating me to another afternoon of aggravation, which has become a tradition for me on Sundays. My daughter walked in just as the umpire called Mattingly out on strikes.

"You idiot!" I shouted. "Mattingly knows the strike zone better than you! If he takes the pitch, it's a ball!"

"Why are you yelling at the TV?" Jackie teased. "I don't think he can hear you." Smart-aleck kids these days.

I calmed myself down. "It's a beautiful day, sweetheart," I said. "Why not ride your bike instead of your father?" She didn't budge. She was having too much fun with me.

"Whenever you watch the game, you get so upset. Why not just stop watching? Do you like getting so angry?"

I had to think about that one. "No, but if I stopped watching I'd be unhappy too," I explained. "The Yankees are a part of my life. They always have been. I can't just stop watching them."

"Are they as important as me and mommy?" she tested.

"Mommy and me, dear," I corrected, showing the teacher in me, "and that's not what I meant. There's no comparison. If I had to, I could forget the Yankees. I love you and your mother and couldn't live without either of you. I just meant that I've been following the Yankees since I was your age, and I guess I'm just used to it. Besides, I really enjoy it, even though it may not always appear that way. It's like when you play video games with your friends. Sometimes you get upset when you lose, but you still keep playing."

"But you always tell me I should play for the fun of playing, not just to try to win," she answered slyly.

"You're right, dear. Maybe I should try to be more . . ."

Just then, Hensley Meulens struck out on a pitch above his eyes. "Yeah! Go ahead, Merrill! Keep Kevin Maas on the bench!" I screamed.

"Bye, Daddy!" Jackie shouted over my yelling, while exiting.

When the Yankees lost to the Dodgers in the 1981 World Series, it was their last post-season appearance. As of this writing, they're not getting any closer. It looks like there may be more frustrating times ahead for the players and fans alike. But the recent dry spell hasn't been the same as the one in the sixties and seventies. Throughout many of the seasons since 1981, the Yanks have been competitive, if not winners. With the likes of Guidry, Dave Winfield, Don Baylor, Rickey Henderson, Randolph, and Mattingly, the team has finished second several times. Only in the last few years have they been out of the pennant race rather early. The Bombers have been losing, but it's been interesting.

The years between 1965 and 1975 tested the patience and loyalty of Yankee fans more than any time before or since. Many didn't pass the test, switching their allegiance to the Mets or simply not following them, accounting for the poor attendance figures during the Michael Burke period. Steinbrenner loyalists can argue that during the losing eighties, the fans never stopped going to the ball park.

I wasn't one of those fans who quit on them. I kept rooting for the Yanks as I do today. I kept going to the ball park, although I don't go as often these days, with my family occupying most of my free time. And I hated the Mets for being the other team in town, which I still do today.

It was hard. The Yanks, as Ogle put it, were an ordinary team, boring to watch most of the time. In spite of what I try to teach my daughter, I like to win or be on the side of a winner, as does everyone. It's difficult to watch a game knowing your team has little chance of winning. That's the feeling Yankee fans had back then. It's what we're beginning to experience in the nineties, but it's still different because the Yanks aren't expected to win the way they used to. We've become accustomed to the idea that the team is just one of the pack, in a game in which no team dominates for a lengthy period of time. The dynasty days are over.

The majesty of Mantle, the miracles of Murcer, the personality of Pepi, the superiority of Stottlemyre, the work of White, and the motivation of Munson—they're what kept me loyal to the Yankees. If one of them left, I had others to keep me going.

It might seem easier to switch to the Mets, who are usually in the thick of things during the chase for the championship. But I won't let that happen to me. The Mets never had the Mick!

EPILOGUE

WHEN I TOLD MY RELATIVES AND friends about this book, some were surprised that I hadn't written on a different subject. Knowing I had a B.A. in political science, some thought a book about the revolutionary changes that have taken place in the Soviet Union and Eastern Europe or the ever-present turmoil in the Middle East would be more challenging. Others felt that since I had been a teacher for twenty years, research on improved educational techniques for inner-city kids or the effects of single-parent home life on school children would be more interesting.

My answer to them would be that there is no subject more important to write about than sports. It's bad enough living in a world filled with corrupt, power-hungry political pirates, or where kids in the big cities of the United States have as much chance of learning as Reggie had of striking out less than a hundred times in a season. Why bother?

Why write about madmen leaders who abuse their power and somehow manage to keep it no matter how many innocent lives are lost? Why write about how our leaders ignore environmental concerns and jeopardize the future of the young and innocent? Why write about the crime rampant in the streets, where vigilante justice is praised by citizens disgusted with the failure of their frustrated law enforcement officials? Why write about an irresponsible minority leader who excuses hoodlum activities by members of his race and is not shouted down as the clown he is by those who once cried for *equal* justice? Why write about the impossibility of teaching children about the importance of getting an education in a community where drug dealers terrify and corrupt innocent minds and families, making survival the *real* priority? Why write about young delinquents who disrupt classrooms, bullying and victimizing conscientious, hard-working students while teachers and principals are prevented from removing them because these hooligans have the "right" to a public education that cannot be denied?

We read and hear about enough serious goings-on each day in the news. The less we have to remind ourselves about the dangers facing us and future generations, the better. A book about baseball is more fun, and a book about the great sports organization whose players meant so much to me in my youth is much more self-fulfilling. I'm happy to have written it. I hope it brings some happiness to everyone who reads it.

INDEX

157

References in **boldface** refer to photographs